'Gave me a new-found confidence...won me £12000 of work...helped me gain more friends – all in 3 weeks. Give me more James Borg. You are a bloody genius!'

Amazon reviewer

'Persuaded? We were. Buy it.'
Management Today magazine (Voted 'best of its kind')

'This is a handy readable guide... The author persuaded me to review this book. Damn, he is good.'

Jeremy Vine, *The Times*

Winner of 'Best of the Rest' award in the "800 CEO – Read Business Book of the Year Awards" 2009 (USA).

Short-listed for the 'BAA Best Non-Fiction Travel Read' 2009 award.

D0418005

Persuasion

PEARSON

At Pearson, we believe in learning – all kinds of learning for all kinds of people. Whether it's at home, in the classroom or in the workplace, learning is the key to improving our life chances.

That's why we're working with leading authors to bring you the latest thinking and the best practices, so you can get better at the things that are important to you. You can learn on the page or on the move, and with content that's always crafted to help you understand quickly and apply what you've learned.

If you want to upgrade your personal skills or accelerate your career, become a more effective leader or more powerful communicator, discover new opportunities or simply find more inspiration, we can help you make progress in your work and life.

Pearson is the world's leading learning company. Our portfolio includes the Financial Times, Penguin, Dorling Kindersley, and our educational business, Pearson International.

Every day our work helps learning flourish, and wherever learning flourishes, so do people.

To learn more please visit us at: www.pearson.com/uk

Persuasion

The art of influencing people

4th edition

JAMES BORG

PEARSON

Harlow, England • London • New York • Boston • San Francisco • Toronto • Sydney
Auckland • Singapore • Hong Kong • Tokyo • Seoul • Taipei • New Delhi
Cape Town • São Paulo • Mexico City • Madrid • Amsterdam • Munich • Paris • Milan

Pearson Education Limited
Edinburgh Gate
Harlow CM20 2JE
United Kingdom
Tel: +44 (0)1279 623623
Web: www.pearson.com/uk

First published in Great Britain in 2004 (print)
Second edition published 2007 (print)
Third edition published 2010 (print)
Fourth edition published 2013 (print and electronic)

© James Borg 2004, 2007, 2010 (print)
© James Borg 2013 (print and electronic)

The right of James Borg to be identified as author of this work has been asserted by him
in accordance with the Copyright, Designs and Patents Act 1988.

Pearson Education is not responsible for the content of third-party internet sites.

ISBN: 978-1-292-00449-5 (print)
        978-1-292-00453-2 (PDF)
        978-1-292-00720-5 (eText)
        978-1-292-00452-5 (ePub)

British Library Cataloguing-in-Publication Data
A catalogue record for the print edition is available from the British Library

Library of Congress Cataloging-in-Publication Data
A catalog record for the print edition is available from the Library of Congress

10 9 8 7 6 5 4 3 2 1
17 16 15 14 13

Cartoons illustrations: Bill Piggins

Print edition typeset in 9.75/13pt Janson LT Std by 30
Print edition printed and bound in Great Britain by Henry Ling, at the Dorset Press,
Dorchester, Dorset.

NOTE THAT ANY PAGE CROSS-REFERENCES REFER TO THE PRINT EDITION

Contents

1 The power of persuasion
How empathy and sincerity work wonders for you 1

2 Being a good listener
Why listening is so crucial 13

3 Attention please
Keeping attention where you want it 31

4 Mind your body language
How to read non-verbal signals from others and send out the right ones 53

5 Memory magic
The impact of good recall and simple tips to improve your memory 83

About the author

James Borg spends his working time as a business consultant and coach and also conducts personal development and business skills workshops covering memory improvement, persuasion, body language awareness and 'mind control'.

With an academic background in economics and psychology, his career spans the spectrum of advertising, sales, marketing, work psychology, training and journalism. He appears on BBC radio and contributes to national newspapers and magazines. In 2009 he was chosen as a *Harvard Business Review* contributor. He still finds time to pursue travel and sports journalism which he became involved with early on in his career.

He is also the author of the award-winning bestsellers *Body Language* and *Mind Power*, the other two books that form the 'trilogy'.

Foreword

Sir John Harvey-Jones MBE

In a world of a continuous barrage of information, the ability to create the bridge of mutual understanding is increasingly more important and more difficult.

Real communication involves trust, integrity and empathy.

This book tells you how to develop and apply these skills.

It should be on every individual's bookshelf.

Sir John Harvey-Jones (1924–2008) was Britain's best-known and admired businessman.

His achievements as chairman of ICI were legendary, where, under his leadership, the giant organization turned a loss of £200 million into £1 billion profit in just 30 months.

For three years running he came top in a 'captains of British industry' award, and he shot to fame as the star of the BAFTA award-winning BBC television series Troubleshooter *which ran between 1990 and 2000. This was the first television 'reality' business pro-gramme and paved the way for more recent ones. The author of several books, including the number-one bestseller* Making It Happen, *in his later years he was one of the country's foremost business speakers.*

Publisher's acknowledgements

WITH ONE LOOK from SUNSET BOULEVARD. Lyrics by Don Black and Christopher Hampton with contributions by Amy Powers. Music by Andrew Lloyd Webber. © Copyright 1993 The Really Useful Group Ltd. All Rights Reserved. International Copyright Secured; Lyrics from *If You Could Read My Mind* by Gordon Lightfoot, © 1969, 1970 (Copyrights Renewed) by EARLY MORNING MUSIC, a division of EMP LTD. All Rights Reserved. Used by Permission of ALFRED PUBLISHING CO., INC., Early Morning Productions Ltd and Mushroom Music Publishing; Lyrics from *I Remember It Well* (from "Gigi") by ALAN JAY LERNER, music by FREDERICK LOEWE © 1957, 1958 (Copyrights Renewed) CHAPPELL & CO., Inc. All Rights Reserved. Used by permission of ALFRED PUBLISHING CO., INC. and Warner Chappell Music Limited; Text from 'Commons Sketch: Under pressure, Chancellor clunking fist almost flunked' by Andrew Gimson, 18 April 2007, *The Daily Telegraph*. © Telegraph Media Group Limited.

In some instances we have been unable to trace the owners of copyright material and we would appreciate any information that would enable us to do so.

Introduction

The power of persuasion is maybe the ultimate source of advantage in life and work. It can be the critical separation factor between the successful and the rest. We all know people who are incredibly persuasive: whatever the situation, somehow they always seem to be able to get others to agree with them, to go with their ideas or to do what they want them to. With some people it seems to be utterly effortless. Maybe they are so well versed in persuasive skills that it *is* effortless.

But the good news for the rest of us is that persuasiveness can be learned and mastered.

In every area of your life you've been involved with trying to move people – almost on a daily basis – to accept your point of view or request. It started early on as an infant, and as you grew older all that changed was the magnitude of the tasks that you were faced with. My interest in the power of persuasion began very early in life when I became fascinated by the psychology of magic (especially mind-reading) and was accepted as one of the youngest members of the Magic Circle.

Good magicians are masters of what are often loosely called 'people skills'. When psychologists were studying the broad area of persuasion and noting how we are all practitioners of this art (every day of our lives), some of them came to an interesting conclusion: they felt that of all the 'persuasive' tasks carried out by human beings, the magician's task was the most difficult. Why? Because they had to 'persuade' their audience (of one or many) to *suspend their disbelief* and **believe** that a miracle had taken place in front of their eyes (whether it was the revealing of a chosen playing card, witnessing the disappearance or production of an object, or a mind-reading miracle).

They observed that first of all the magician would get and then control the audience's **attention** (whether it was one person or hundreds). They would use the 'right' **words**, **listen** carefully to any volunteers (giving due respect) and get them to **remember** the things they wanted them to remember (often through the 'power of suggestion'). At the same time, they would work out what **'type'** of person they were dealing with; inject some humour into the proceedings (to induce relaxation); 'read' the other person by observing their **body language**; and ultimately get the audience to 'trust' and feel favourably disposed towards them. All of which is designed to do one thing: persuade the audience to suspend their disbelief (and be entertained). *A good demonstration of people/communication skills in action!* But just like in everyday life, the most successful ones are those who deploy these skills effectively and have highly developed powers of persuasion.

In the many years I've spent in the business world, I've realized the huge advantage of being able to bring people along to our way of thinking. Every day, at work – and, of course, in your personal life – you come into contact with people who need to understand your point of view, either for you to help *them* or for them to help *you*. Equally, you need to understand their point of view. We need to be able to persuade others to our way of thinking and 'read' how they are thinking.

In short, the power of persuasion is that elusive formula that we wish we could get our hands on to make life smoother for us. We could define it as this: *any message that attempts to influence people's opinions, attitudes or actions.*

If there is a magic formula then the concoction is the application all of these techniques and skills *together*. This will help you to take people from **'point A to point B,'** because persuasion is a 'process'.

This book is the result of my own experiences over many successful years in advertising, sales, marketing, journalism, work psychology and coaching – all underpinned by applied behavioural and social psychology research.

As these are all tried and tested techniques, my aim has been to simplify the process of persuasion by showing its application in 'real-world' situations. The book will show you how to put yourself and your thoughts across convincingly and how to 'read' other people more effectively; and in so doing to allow you to be more persuasive and for people to trust and feel favourably disposed towards you.

It will make you more aware of your senses and help you to bring out the 'sixth sense' that lies dormant within all of us. Leonardo da Vinci astutely observed that the average person *'looks without seeing, listens without hearing, touches without feeling, eats without tasting, moves without physical awareness, inhales without awareness of odour or fragrance, and talks without thinking.'* Does that sound like a fair assessment of most of the human race (or you!)? Certainly, if I had to pinpoint in a phrase what separates the master 'persuaders' from the rest, it's that they have an ability to understand what is going on in the other person's head.

The purpose of this book? As with the other two books that form part of the 'trilogy': to *inform, educate* and *entertain*.

An important point that I can't stress enough is that 'persuasion' in this book, used in this way, is entirely **positive**. It works for your benefit – and for that of the people you are dealing with. You won't have success every time, but by honing these skills and your own self-awareness, you'll find that you increase your success rate significantly and forge better relationships. *More and more research confirms that both in our working and personal lives it is persuasive skills that separate those who succeed from those who are less successful.*

So this is a book about **person-to-person** persuasion, which after all is the starting point for most successful interactions. Life is all about people – and how we deal with them individually.

It's probably quite different to most books you've read on a related subject matter. You may have come across some of the ideas before, but not dealt with in a 'real-world' context.

By the end of the book, I hope that you will come to the conclusion that it is you (the person) who is persuasive and not the techniques that you use. It's not so much about defining what you actually do, but rather the way you *are*. You are persuasive because of the way that you have integrated the core skills and various modes of behaviour – as outlined over the chapters – into your life. Self-awareness is key.

As my economics professor used to say, paraphrasing J.K. Galbraith: 'The world divides into just two types: those of us who don't know and those of us who *don't know* that we don't know.'

This book is for both!

– James Borg

'Ever notice that *"what the hell"* is always the right decision?'

Marilyn Monroe

Chapter

1

'An ounce of intuition is worth a pound of tuition.'

Unknown

The power of persuasion

How empathy and sincerity work wonders for you

- Aristotle's art of persuasion
- Empathy
- Sincerity

So what's this book about?

Many years ago when playwright Tom Stoppard was asked what his first play was about, he replied, 'It's *about* to make me very rich.'

This book may very well do this for you. More than that, it is essentially about an awareness of communicating in a manner that will increase your persuasive skills and lead to significant gains in your professional and personal life.

Inspector Clouseau (Peter Sellers) (to hotel clerk at reception): 'Does your dog bite?'

Hotel clerk: 'No.'

Inspector Clouseau (to dog): 'Nice doggie.'

Dog bites Clouseau.

Inspector Clouseau: 'A-aaagh . . . I thought you said it didn't bite.'

Hotel clerk: 'That is not my dog.'

Peter Sellers as Inspector Clouseau, *The Pink Panther*

At work and at home, all of us will try to get a point across or get somebody to agree to a course of action, many times every day. There's always a need to win over other people for one reason or another. The more effective you are at communicating, the greater your chances of being successful at persuasion.

3

Aristotle's art of persuasion

Our basic human values have not changed that much over the centuries, as it was the philosopher Aristotle (384–322 BC) over 2,300 years ago who laid the groundwork for successful communication. His is the most influential theory regarding persuasion. For him, persuasion was an art.

It was **'the art of getting people to do something they wouldn't ordinarily do if you didn't ask'**.

He observed that, as social animals, all humans were called upon to persuade fellow human beings almost on a daily basis. All persuasive situations sought to attain the goal of taking the audience from the starting point, which he called point A, and moving them along to point B (your objective). This shifting of attitude is what he called **persuasion**. At point A, the person/audience is uninterested and resistant to your ideas or proposals. So they have to have an understanding of the views you are putting forward and, more importantly, believe the message. Aristotle argued that any persuasive speech – whether it be to one or hundreds of people – can be entertaining, thought-provoking, eloquent or whatever, but that was not the point of the message. Its sole purpose was to move the audience to point B.

To be persuasive, he spoke of three different types of proof that were used by persuasive speakers:

- *Ethos* (ethical – character and reputation)
- *Pathos* (emotional appeal)
- *Logos* (logical)

The best persuasive messages strive to blend all three in order to achieve the goal of moving people from A to B.

Ethos relates to the speaker and his or her character as revealed through the communication. For the message to be believable, there had to be 'source credibility' – this is something that exists in the minds of the listeners. So it's the trustworthiness that the speaker had in the audience's eyes. It relates to the person and refers to the *sincerity* that exudes from the individual.

Pathos relates to the *emotions* felt by the audience. As Aristotle put it, '*Persuasion may come through the hearers when the speech stirs their emotions.*' In other words, it was essential to appeal to the emotions felt by your listeners in order to be persuasive. In short, you had to have *empathy*.

Logos refers to the actual *words* used by the speaker. Choice of words and use of stories, quotations and facts Aristotle cited as being important in moving the audience over to your point of view.

Take a look at your style of presenting a viewpoint or argument to your 'audience'. Do you use all three elements? Observe other people and how they use them. When you're dealing with others, note what the *dominant* element is in their conversations (e.g. they may use a lot of pathos), then try to match them.

For Aristotle, logos was the primary element, with ethos and pathos as secondary. **In the present day, there's good reason for voting ethos as the number one**, followed by pathos and then logos. Think how important the issue of trust (ethos) is to politicians and how we don't believe anything they say if they have lied to us or not fulfilled promises. All their pathos (emotion) and logos (words) mean nothing. Of course, this is not confined to politics; it also applies to us in our dealings with people in everyday life.

Assuming that trust has been established at the outset (ethos) Aristotle was telling us was that when striving to get through to the other person we have to use a combination of **logic** and **emotion**.

There are two routes to the persuasion process: what we would now call the subconscious and the conscious mind. As you would imagine, logic deals mainly with the **conscious** mind. The other person concentrates on the facts and assesses the situation on an intellectual level before coming to a rational decision: in other words, am I persuaded. Think of people you know, or deal with, that place great importance initially on the 'processing' of facts in order to decide whether to take the next mental step.

For others it is the **subconscious** that rules. This person would assess the information being given by the 'persuader' based on their emotional feel of the situation and their intuition. If they feel well-disposed towards the other person, and they've satisfied the 'ethos' element (trustworthiness), they'll make a decision based on this primary feeling. Then they'll look to *back-up* the decision by going over the facts. (But in a world of too much information we can sometimes be overwhelmed with 'paralysis by analysis' – too many facts which may cause us to defer a decision, mentally). If these facts are satisfactory then the person may be open to persuasion.

Repeated studies show that – in the main – it's the subconscious (or emotional) element that is the *primary* reason for making a decision. So even though we're conscious human beings, our instinct and gut-feeling drives us to make decisions.

But logic is still important, as we then 'validate' the decision with the logical element; essential, because *feelings come and go* – as we know in romantic affairs of the heart! (When we discuss 'types' in Chapter 10 you'll have an idea as to the optimum balance to use in certain situations.)

Empathy

More than two millennia on and the observations of the wise philosopher still hold true. Aristotle's pathos – having the perception to ascertain the true feelings of people that you deal with, or **empathy** as it's better known these days – is at the heart of most successful relationships.

Let's provide a definition for this term as it is the bedrock of all successful communication:

'Empathy is the ability to identify and understand the other person's feelings, ideas and situation.'

It's listening with your heart as well as your head. It's the ability to read emotions in others. It's being able to experience another person's perspective. It's the next best thing to the powers of ESP and reading minds.

From an emotional point of view, even if you have not experienced a similar state of affairs, you are still able to empathize and know how another person feels. It motivates us to search for outcomes that not only leave us feeling good, but also leave the other person in the same frame of mind. It's a kind of detached involvement.

Application of this important quality is essential in all areas of life: it's helpful in all aspects of work; politicians yearn to project this quality; parents have to develop this skill to a fine degree; and if you're trying to improve on your success with the opposite sex – see what happens when you don't have it.

Some people have this innate sense to a very high degree. So they use it successfully. They're almost able to predict how another person will react to something. **They put themselves on a similar wavelength, so they know what to say and how to say it.** They try to read the minds of those they are dealing with.

When you look at the behaviours and mindsets of the most successful people around – in any field – it's apparent that they have a great understanding of the role of empathy. It's not something to be faked. Other people know when it's genuine. When they feel there's a sincere desire by a person to *feel* how *they* feel – understand what it's like to be in their shoes – an initial rapport develops. This, of course, increases the chances of them being open to your ideas and suggestions.

It's fair to say that society is such that we are almost conditioned to expect that people are ultimately trying to persuade us to do or believe something for *their* reasons – with not much concern for ours – so when we come across people who show sincere empathy, we can't help but be receptive.

Think about people in your own life that you feel comfortable with and like and admire. Chances are, these people have great empathy – probably something you hadn't thought about or bothered to analyse in the past.

Sincerity

Aristotle's ethos or 'source credibility' of the speaker relates to the **sincerity** of the individual, as we noted earlier. Sincerity is essential if you're going to develop empathy. But being sincere is not enough. Ultimately empathy is based on trust.

Think about it in terms of general relationships. The first crisis that often occurs in any relationship is when two individuals no longer trust each other. Everything that a person does either *promotes* or *lessens* the trust within a relationship. It is not a stable personality trait that we possess, as it is changing constantly.

To put it more succinctly: trust occurs *between* people and not *within* people. Some people are more trusting than others, and some people are inherently more trustworthy; but it's the *conveying* of it to the other person that's most important. This is an important psychological point that we tend to overlook.

Some people emit true sincerity without effort, and so the other person's trust level is high. If you show genuine sincerity – that you actually care about someone's problems or concerns, be it a friend, relative, work colleague, client or whoever – you're elevating yourself to a higher plane. Conversations take on a different tone. The other person is more receptive to your questions and tells you more. **This helps you steer a discussion in the direction you want**. A certain amount of trust has been established. (Remember: trust exists in relationships, not in someone's personality.) It's being trustworthy that advances a relationship.

The more supportive you are of the other person, the more likely it is that they will disclose their thoughts, ideas and feelings to you. And it's a circular relationship, because the more trustworthy you are in response to these 'self-disclosures', the deeper and more personal will be the thoughts that the person shares with you. This occurs as much in a business context as it does in private life.

Empathy + Sincerity → Persuasion (ESP)

Researchers in the behavioural sciences in recent years have noted the two qualities that time and time again have been shown to enhance the communication process and therefore an individual's success in winning over people to their point of view. **The two qualities are empathy and sincerity**.

More recently, there has been much analysis and publicity given to the concept of **'emotional intelligence'** as a predictor of success, highlighting these core qualities. This is 2,300 years after the writings of Aristotle!

It has to be said:

> **No amount of learning or brushing-up of communication skills on their own without the core virtues of empathy and sincerity to back them up will succeed in the long term.**

It requires bringing out our two types of intelligences, which psychologists refer to as follows:

- *Interpersonal intelligence*: an understanding of other people – how they feel, their likes and dislikes, their motivations. The person with this ability can almost predict how others will act and is therefore able to interact with them effectively and be very persuasive. In life, you'll notice that successful politicians, salespeople, psychotherapists and people with highly developed social skills possess this kind of intelligence.

- *Intrapersonal intelligence*: the ability to have insight into our own thought processes, feelings and emotions, and an awareness of the causes and consequences of our actions, which in turn allows us to make the right decision.

Possession of these qualities enables us to get inside the minds of other people and be effective in our communication with them.

Since communication is transmitted through our *attitudes* as well as the application of various methods and techniques, mere competence in the use of these skills is not sufficient. This can not be stressed enough.

Despite their importance, the techniques described throughout this book will promote good relationships and successful influencing only when backed up by the core virtues of empathy and sincerity. The techniques on their own are insufficient in the formation of productive relationships. So, ultimately:

> **Empathy + Sincerity → Persuasion**

They are the building blocks for successful persuasion.

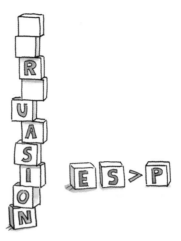

For some people, the word 'persuasion' has ominous under-tones. But throughout this book, when we use the term, we're talking about the art of gentle persuasion – subtle techniques that work on the mind to produce a desirable result for both parties. Moving people from point A to point B. We all have an aversion to the feeling of having been manipulated. That's not what this book is about. It's about communicating in a way that results in favourable outcomes.

The book begins with listening, which complements empathy as a core interpersonal intelligence (or 'emotional intelligence') and relationship skill, and is perhaps the most important skill to master for successful relationships.

As to how crucial the process of effective listening is to our own existence, this was summed up succinctly by the communications expert and psychologist Carl Rogers:

'Man's inability to communicate is a result of his failure to listen effectively, skilfully and with understanding to another person.'

Chapter

2

'We lived for days on nothing but food and water.'

W.C. Fields

Being a good listener
Why listening is so crucial

- Running 'tapes' in your own head
- I hear what you say
- We think much faster than we can speak
- Paraphrasing

Of all the aspects of communication, listening is the most important. Now that might not sound like good news – most of us prefer talking to listening, after all. Comments like 'she's a good listener' are often made about people who don't have much to say for themselves. Stop and think about it though.

Think about somebody you know who isn't a good listener. Who, in fact, never seems to listen to anything you say. Frustrating, isn't it? And how does it make you feel about that person? Chances are they will have a hard time persuading you as you are too busy feeling annoyed because they never listen.

Powerful persuasion begins with the ability to hear what others are saying. And listening is about far more than being quiet when somebody else speaks. In the divorce courts and in the workplace, a breakdown is often attributed to poor listening. If listening is carried out effectively, it creates and improves personal and business relationships. In every situation in life, *effective* listening will help you to understand another person's thoughts, feelings and actions.

When people are accused of being poor listeners, it is usually done behind their backs. So they remain unaware of this major failing, which can lose them friends, work colleagues and business clients.

How do you rate as a listener? Being a bad one is a very serious sin of which most people are guilty. They only *think* they listen. The compulsion to speak in very many cases devalues the function of listening.

Fact: most people prefer talking to listening (and, unfortunately, they usually exercise this preference). In order to be persuasive, mastering the art of listening (as opposed to *hearing*, which we'll discuss later) is critical to success.

Active listening is difficult. It requires a lot of concentration. You have to be alert. But it has to be mastered. It is fundamental to learning. The sad thing is that we were never taught at school about the importance of listening skills. Even now, more emphasis is placed on trigonometry than on listening.

A much-cited study by Paul Rankin on how much time people spent in various types of communication showed interesting results. In a typical day the average person:

Listened: 45% of the time
Spoke: 30%
Read: 16%
Wrote: 9%

In our working life, listening is highly prized as a desirable interpersonal skill. People are impressed with good listening in others, even though they might not feel they should make the effort themselves. Over in the US when a large computer company decided to train its employees in listening, and sent them on courses throughout the country, the employees' feedback was that as well as it helping them in their working arena, it was instrumental in improving relationships dramatically at home.

You often hear of somebody talking too much. Nobody could be accused of *listening* too much ('Gosh – I just couldn't stop that person listening – made me miss my train . . .'). It's surprising what people will tell you if you're a good listener. Think how it works among friends and acquaintances on a social level. What were you like the last time you bumped into your neighbour in the street, or when you were having dinner with friends? In families, you'll constantly hear that there's a listening problem. Beleaguered parents will say that the children don't listen, while children will be exasperated because their parents don't listen to them. Since listening is a sign of affirmation, it promotes self-esteem; the opposite usually occurs if there is a breakdown.

In business it's no different. People are drawn to a good listener. There may be a definite appeal in being able to talk to somebody outside the internal politics of their own company who listens objectively. A person bogged down in the red tape of their own position may relish the therapeutic satisfaction of getting something off their chest to an outsider.

This little rhyme speaks volumes:

'His thoughts were slow,
His words were few,
And never made to glisten,
But he was a joy
Wherever he went
You should have heard him listen.'

It pays good dividends if you listen. It can establish you as a 'friend'. And that makes for more mutual understanding in a business relationship.

Besides, if you listen carefully, you pick up all sorts of information about the idiosyncrasies of an organization – and the individual you are dealing with. People who are poor listeners often see listening as a passive – and therefore unproductive – activity. Their ego gets in the way. They feel the need to be talking in order to make any impact with the other person.

Observe people in internal meetings in the workplace and you'll see the talk–talk–talk syndrome with a vengeance. There are those who continually interrupt with superfluous remarks.

It makes them believe that they're contributing. They'll miss important points through butting in. And they'll ask questions to which they already know the answers. But they're communicating, they feel, because they're *talking*. How wrong they are! Attentive listening is also part of communication.

You'll quite often see the above scenario in sales situations. Talking long and loud doesn't always equate with having personality; it is often a substitute for it.

Running 'tapes' in your own head

There's only one way to listen productively: try to remove all distractions from your mind so you can concentrate on the speaker – easier said than done! **Such distractions come from your thoughts, senses and emotions.** 'Tapes' in your own head. Preoccupation or lack of interest impedes effective listening.

If you're not interested in what the speaker has to offer, then you'll have an aversion to listening. Preoccupation with something can be a barrier too. For example, if someone has just bumped into the back of your car, the nuisance of it keeps coming back to you.

The environment can also influence how well we listen. Have you ever tried to have a meaningful discussion with somebody when there's a TV set blaring in the background? Your requests to have it turned off because you want to discuss something might meet with a reply such as, 'It's OK, I can listen even if it's on.' You might achieve a compromise with the other person, agreeing to turn the sound off and leave only the picture on. It doesn't work. You're still distracted by the visual 'noise', even though the auditory interference has been eliminated. Noise can come from all sources. It's difficult to concentrate in a meeting if there are roadworks going on outside. Equally, you could be in a seminar and miss the first 20 minutes of what is said through being absorbed in a beautiful oil painting hung over the fireplace (visual noise again).

I often use what I call the 'W.C. Fields test' if I want to test somebody's listening skills. There's his old quip: '*We lived for days on nothing but food and water.*' In conversation, if I sense somebody isn't listening, I'll throw in this statement relating to a fictitious scenario and the responses are quite amusing. They range from 'Oh, how awful' and 'How on earth did you manage?' to 'That's terrible', 'Oh, really?' and 'What happened?' Then there are the people who actually 'listen' and respond with a smile or laugh as the words sink in. Try it. You'll find it interesting (and amusing).

So, who are you trying to kid when you claim to be a good listener? Listening isn't merely saying nothing while the other person is talking. It's deriving *meaning* from what's said. And that's what people find difficult. They think it's just hearing.

I hear what you say

There's a lot of confusion and discord perpetrated in our daily lives because of a lack of distinction between *hearing* and *listening*. OK – you've always assumed the two terms to be interchangeable (I hear what you say!). But in fact the two terms are wholly different.

Hearing is a sensory activity. It's a **physiological** process in which our auditory connections transmit information to the brain – through, of course, the ears.

Listening is something different. It denotes the process of interpreting and understanding. It means deriving meaning from what has been heard – it is a **psychological** process.

We've all probably been guilty of being challenged at not listening to what's been said and then meekly repeated the words back verbatim (whilst being *amazed* and *relieved* that we haven't fluffed our lines).

Her: 'Look, you've got to get the car serviced in the next few days – we've got that long drive down to Mum's on Christmas Day.'

Him (absorbed in a World Cup rugby match on television)

Her: 'You didn't listen to a word I said, did you?'

Him: 'What? Yeah, course I did. We've got to get the car serviced in the next few days because of the long drive down to your mum's on Christmas Day. OK. I'll get it serviced as soon as Christmas is over.'

Getting the lines right (hearing) doesn't look as though it will work in this instance! So, effective listening is really a combination of the two activities, which results in deriving meaning and understanding from the speaker's words. It's not easy. It's truly a skill.

We think much faster than we can speak

There's a major obstacle to effective listening that we all have to contend with: we can think much faster than anyone can speak. Tests have shown that:

● we talk at between 120 and 150 words per minute;
● we think at the rate of 600 to 800 words per minute.

Result: since we can *think* at approximately **four to five times** the rate that somebody is *speaking*, we tend to think of other things and not just about what is being said.

Of course, the figures vary, but the fundamental point is that the listener is always **ahead** of the person doing the talking. The implications of this are evident. When listening to people, the radio, television or whatever, your mind has time to wander away from the words being spoken. So you lose concentration. And if you start thinking about something and it takes you over, you'll blot out the other noise and thus switch off. You may look as though you're listening, but you're not actually hearing anything.

Since all communication between individuals essentially moves the relationship either forwards or backwards, or keeps it the same, the way you listen and respond to other people is paramount in promoting the relationship. If you listen empathically, you're giving out the signal: 'I'm interested in everything that you're saying and I'm eager to understand your point of view'; if you fail to listen and respond in the right way, you're saying the opposite.

So how do we get the best out of the speaker by showing that we're listening in the right fashion?

Don't interrupt

Because thoughts formulate faster than speech, there's a strong temptation to interrupt the other person. It's a sign that you're not listening, or that you're eager to sidetrack the speaker's line of reasoning (in favour of your own), or that you are one of the many people who enjoy talking more than listening. Whatever the reason, you may antagonize the other person. They're less likely to listen intently to you (when they've got to do the listening) if you cut them off midstream. The spontaneity is gone once you've interrupted. Consider this example:

First neighbour to second neighbour: 'You know, I've been thinking about the problem of your new extension blocking the light from our bedroom. I know it's been approved by the council and you've got planning permission. I don't want us to fall out . . .'

Second neighbour (interrupting): 'Look, it's OK, I've been to see the architect and I've told him to reduce the height. It's sorted out. Sarah didn't want any bad feeling. Neither did I.'

First neighbour: 'But I meant . . .'

Second neighbour: 'It's fine, honestly. Don't think any more about it. I've got to dash – I'll get stuck in the traffic on the M25. Bye.'

Well, if the second neighbour had listened without interrupting, events would have taken a different course. His neighbour was going to say: 'We're having a loft conversion done – been toying with the idea for years. Sue suggested we make that our new bedroom, as it's much bigger and faces south, and so your extension won't be a problem for us.'

Take a moment to think how you feel the next time you are interrupted during a conversation. Did it please you? Were you annoyed? Were their sentences better than yours?

If you recognise yourself as someone who engages in this kind of behaviour it might be worthwhile to think back to some of these instances for a moment. Did it work? Meaning, did it produce the required outcome? Did the person like you better for the interruption or could you tell from the body language that they weren't very pleased?

What about when people interrupt you? Can you think back to a few instances? We're not talking about those moments when people interrupt us (and we, them) through *excitement* of the topic being discussed ('Yeah, we went to see that last month in Windsor as well – great!'). There's a difference. This kind of interruption is usually **transient** and allows the speaker to continue immediately. The **irritating** interruption causes the speaker to lose flow and rhythm (*and sometimes the conversation is taken over by the other person*).

Don't finish the other person's sentences

As we saw in the example of the two neighbours, one person's interjection turned out to be detrimental to his cause – he'd have been much better off if he had kept quiet and let his neighbour finish. Another irritating habit – if it's done repeatedly – is to finish the speaker's sentences. Consider the following:

Client: 'And so this time I want to avoid any . . .'

Designer (interrupting): 'Further catastrophe?'

Client: 'Er, yes. That's right.'

Designer: 'Don't worry. We'll pull out all the stops.'

You can do this occasionally, but don't make a habit of it. To keep doing it to the same person is not only irritating but also bad psychology, because the speaker will not feel in control of their own ideas.

Filling in words for somebody on the odd occasion can show that you are actually listening and provide feedback that you are attentive, but it can also get in the way of the other person's ego. It may well look as though you're trying to wrestle original thoughts from them and claim them for your own. That renders you suspect and will not help the rapport that you're aiming to establish.

There's another drawback to jumping the gun like this: **you may easily guess the wrong ending**! Perhaps that possibility has never occurred to you, simply because nobody has ever bothered to correct your mistake.

Maybe the other person doesn't want to embarrass you and tell you that you're an idiot who has messed up their line of thought. Because they can't do that, they can't continue with their original point (and it may have been crucial).

The ending that you so kindly supplied (i.e. the wrong one) may implant doubts that never previously existed. For example:

Geoff (the client): 'I'm happy to do business with you – it's a couple of years now, I think, since we dealt with you – but I want to make sure . . .'

You (interrupting): '. . . that you don't get the wrong consignment like you did the last time, and have to wait another three weeks.'

Ouch!

What Geoff was actually going to say was: 'I want to make sure . . . that the purchase order form that we'll send you gives the different delivery locations for each batch.'

What's happened is that the client is alerted to the fact that your company messed up the delivery last time, which caused a three-week delay. He may not have known anything about it or may have forgotten. You've just told him. Now he has doubts because late delivery could cost his company a lot of money and bad feeling within the organization. Geoff decides to think about it – 'I'll get back to you.' He never does. Business has been lost because of a throw-away and ill-considered line.

To make matters worse, what your client was actually going to say was to your benefit.

Remember the old adage: **'Better to keep your mouth shut and be thought a fool, than to open it and remove all doubt!'**

Talking over the other person

Another bad habit adopted by many people is talking over the other person while they are speaking. You may think of members of your family, friends or work colleagues who are guilty of this. Your boss may do it to you all the time. It's very common. And it's very irritating when you're on the receiving end. It says: 'I don't care what you're going to say, my story's better than yours' (or bigger and better than yours – remind you of the school playground?). For example:

Anne: 'Did you enjoy the cruise, Charlotte? How was it?'

Charlotte: 'Oh, I can't tell you how much we enjoyed ourselves. Do you know, they had food on each deck at almost all hours, day and night . . .' (what she says next is completely drowned out by the other person) '. . . and then there were midnight buffets and unfortunately we got a touch of food poisoning on . . .'

Anne (talking over her): 'Oh, how wonderful. We went on a fabulous cruise. Now when would that have . . . ? Oh, I know, it must have been ten – no – more like eight and a half years . . .'

Do you recognize this tendency – *one-upping* – in yourself?

Or do you recognize it in other people? We all talk over others to some extent, for various reasons not evident at the time, such as excitement, a desire to show empathy or a desire to 'bring someone down' (if they're obnoxious). If we're aware of it, we can at least try to avoid doing it. It can lose you friends and it can lose you business.

So the message is clear: whether it's you doing the listening or whether you want somebody to listen effectively to what you say, try to avoid or prevent any barriers to productive listening.

Offering advice too soon

This is often a problem when you're eager to help someone, whether it be a friend, a colleague or somebody in a business situation. You want to offer support and help, so you jump into the conversation quickly. The result is that there's an abrupt and premature end to the two-way conversation. If you're the classic 'problem-solving' type, you may be guilty of this; if you're the type that oozes empathy, you may also do this frequently. It comes from a desire to help.

'That's twice he's telephoned at the last minute, saying he has to work late. I'm concerned: the thought crossed my mind that he might be seeing someone else. I don't know whether I'm just being silly . . .'

'Ditch him. He's not worth it.'

'You see, our problem is the staff just don't stay. Maybe after four to six months they . . . I don't know whether it's the attitude of our senior people towards them. Or, I don't know, there could be a few other reasons . . .'

'Don't worry. We vet all applicants thoroughly. Our company's been around for ten years now. I'm sure we can get some stability for you.'

The problem in both of these examples is that the quick response has blocked any further lines of enquiry. Although they hadn't finished, the speakers were cut off, and now the conversation is being guided in the listener's direction. The speakers had more to get off their chest and have been cut short.

Psychologists operating in the field of therapy are coming to realize that all too often clients aren't heard because therapists are doing therapy *to* them rather than *with* them. Instead of listening to what clients are saying and becoming immersed in their conversations, there is a tendency to make up meanings about what they said. Conversational questions arise from a position of not knowing; they involve responsive and active listening and do not come about from a therapist's preconceived theories.

Paraphrasing

Listening empathetically is the key to advancing interpersonal relationships. The technique of paraphrasing is very powerful as it lets the speaker see the ideas (and feelings) they have conveyed from the other person's point of view. When you paraphrase, you are not adding to the message; you are sending back the meaning you received. The listener is effectively telling the speaker, using their own words, what they interpret from what has been said. It is invaluable because:

● The sender is reassured that the listener is trying to understand the basis of their thoughts and feelings, and appreciates being heard.

'Let me just clarify what you're saying. You're a bit concerned about a stranger having your flat keys, and that's the main reason.'

'Yes, exactly.'

'It looks as though what you're saying is you'll place your television advertising budget with us as long as there's no conflict of interest with another client.'

'That's correct.'

● The listener may want to ensure that the sender hears what they have just said (this could be for a positive or a negative reason), as this will give them a clearer perspective of the implications of their current line of thinking.

'At the moment it looks as though you're saying that you want to give up the classes altogether. You realize that if you change your mind later, you'd have to start from scratch again – is that what you want?'

'Well . . . no, I suppose not.'

'Can I just clarify what I think you're saying? You'd like your IT managers to try the system out piecemeal. It would end up costing you four times as much this way. Would that be acceptable to the departmental managers?'

'Mmm . . . that's something to consider.'

- The listener may have found it difficult to gauge the other person's true feelings and needs to try to attain an accurate understanding of what has been said.

'I'd just like to ask you if I've understood this correctly. You want to change departments because the gossiping interferes with your work. That's it, is it?'

'Well, there are other things.'

'Can I just be sure of this in my own mind? It's the fact that he doesn't ever ask how you are that makes you feel this way?'

'No. That's just a small part of it – it's the tip of the iceberg.'

It's a fact of life that people, in making the decision as to whether to go along with our way of thinking, will be using their line of reasoning and not ours. Sometimes they do not even know what their line of reasoning is, so we need to use some empathetic questioning to dig deep and read minds. A lot of this may be based on emotions. Therefore, your natural empathy has to spring into action. We need to listen for the deep meanings in any communication.

We have a much better chance of influencing somebody if we can get to the bottom of their reasoning and make an educated guess at their way of thinking.

I cannot overemphasize the importance of listening in family life, work situations and friendships. It pays enormous dividends. One of the traits of persuasive or charismatic people is that they have this facility not only to feel, but also to look fascinated by what somebody else is saying to them. Most of our life is spent listening. Of course, we want people to listen to us too, so our questions are important, as are getting and holding attention.

At the end of this and subsequent chapters, take a moment to recap on the main points by completing the short quiz in the 'coffee break' section. The first letter has been inserted as an *aide-mémoire*.

Coffee break . . .

☕ Most people prefer t_____ to listening – and they tend to exercise that preference.

☕ We think f_____ times faster than we can speak, so listening to another person is difficult, as we're always a_____ of the listener.

☕ Because our thoughts formulate faster than another person's speech, we tend to i_____ and may lose out in the process.

☕ People are not usually told that they are poor listeners – if it's voiced at all, it is usually b_____ their b_____, resulting in a lack of awareness.

☕ Distractions come from our own t_____, senses and e_____.

☕ Listening empathetically by p_____ is very persuasive and very powerful.

☕ People confuse hearing and listening. Hearing is a s_____ activity. Listening is p_____ and is concerned with deriving m_____ and understanding from what's been heard – the two processes have to work in combination. So, you might be a good hearer and not a good listener after all!

☕ The technique of paraphrasing is powerful as it lets the speaker see the ideas and f_____ that have been c_____ from the o_____ person's point of view.

(Answers and a scoring scale to ascertain your PQ (Persuasion Quotient) are on page 287)

Chapter

3

'*Interviewer (to candidate for a job)*: 'OK then, following on from that . . . if you could have dinner with someone, living or dead, who would you choose?'

Candidate's reply: 'The one that was living, definitely.'

Attention please

Keeping attention where you want it

- Attention breakdowns
- The attention curve
- Ways to win more attention

We want people to listen to our message, so we have to keep our audience – whether it be one or two people or 200 – interested enough to listen. Furthermore, we want to keep their attention. Most of us have short concentration spans, for various reasons. It's very difficult to keep interest level constant. Attention is held only when interest is rising. In the previous chapter, we spoke about the problem of the mind allowing itself to engage in competing thoughts (because we can think at a faster rate than the rate at which a person typically speaks) while seemingly paying attention to something else. Sure, we're 'hearing' – but we're not listening. *Most people assume that the two actions are complementary*. But they're not – as this overheard conversation illustrates:

'What did you do at the weekend, then?'

'Drove down to the coast with the kids, to Brighton, and stayed overnight.'

'Oh, Brighton. I haven't been there for years. Did you take the train?'

'No, I drove there.'

'Did you go on your own?'

Disastrous! The questioner was not truly listening. He edited the conversation until he found a key word that sparked his interest – and then, of course, he missed all the other details. The rest were words he had chosen just not to register. Go on, admit it to yourself. You do it all the time, don't you? At home; when you're with your friends; in shops; at work; when you're interviewing an applicant for a job position; in business meetings; while you're watching television; in the theatre – in fact, *just about wherever you are!*

People fool themselves into thinking that they're good listeners. They're probably good hearers, but that doesn't allow them to take interest in, and thus make use of, what they are told to further their romantic relationships, their friendships or their dealings at work. For example, a woman is talking to her husband, who's sitting in an armchair looking at the television, remote control in hand:

'You *will* mow the lawn for me tomorrow, won't you?'

'What? Oh yes, yes.'

'We've got to get to the theatre by seven, so we ought to leave now.'

'Yes. OK, OK.'

'I was going to wear this dress – d'you think it makes my bottom look big?'

'Yes, yes.'

'What? You think it's big?'

'What? No! I mean no.'

'You just said "yes" to everything. If you'd unglue that remote from your hand . . . You don't listen to anything I say.'

Ouch! What probably makes this situation even worse is that although the woman's partner was looking at the television, he was probably only hearing and not listening to the sound. He was listening to his own thoughts in his head. We're all constantly '**running our own tapes**'.

How can we encourage people to listen to us? How can we gain their attention, keep their attention? By keeping them interested in what we have to say, so that they won't get bored and start listening to themselves.

Actors know very well that their success in the West End, on Broadway, in a local theatre or even in a school play depends first on one thing: maintaining audience attention.

Their aim is to make interest rise for the maximum length of time and to try to prevent it falling. They have to compete with the audience's own mental distractions, let alone any visual distractions. A lapse of attention by a member of the audience during a 'boring' scene may let in all sorts of extraneous thoughts:

'. . . Mmm. I hope the car will be all right parked where it is. It was sticking out from the corner a bit. Not my fault. Why do they need double yellows that far round a corner? They're a bit trigger-happy, those traffic wardens around here. If Sue's aunt hadn't phoned we wouldn't have been late. Why do people always . . . We could have got into the car park if it wasn't for her. Still, it's now a lot nearer than the car park. I hope I can find it later. Oh yes, I know. It's near that pizza place. They do nice pizzas there. Maybe we'll eat there later. I'll phone during the interval and see if they'll reserve a table. Now, where's my mobile phone? It's not in my pocket – I must have dropped it as we came in . . . unless. . . that chap that looked as though he bumped into me deliberately . . . pickpocket . . . why, the thieving, no-good, son-of . . . no wait a minute, I gave it to Sue to put in her handbag before we left home. What's that thing on the edge of the stage? Oh, it's a knife. I wonder if she knows she's got a big hole in her stocking . . . ?'

By the time they try to get back into the swing of the play, they find they've lost interest and it's hard to regain it.

Attention breakdowns

This problem exists all the time in everyday life. Let's take a typical business situation. You're visiting a prospective client's office (this could equally well be a job interview, a consultation with a private doctor in Harley Street or just about any kind of 'meeting' – the problems are still the same). You enter the client's office and take the seat offered. After a few pleasantries you begin your presentation.

- Three minutes into your spiel, the client's telephone rings. 'Do excuse me for a minute,' he says, taking the call.

- After two or three minutes, when he has finished, he turns back to you: 'Now, where were we? I'm sorry. Please carry on.'

- You recall where you left off and continue talking. The client nods as you are speaking and you feel that he's with you. About two minutes later, his secretary walks in. 'Excuse me,' she says to both of you, and then addressing her boss: 'Would you just sign this, please? It's very urgent.'

- He apologizes to you and stares at the cheque. He questions his secretary about a certain point relating to the amount on the cheque. He then asks her to locate some paperwork from the files. She leaves.

- You pick up your thread and afterwards ask the client some questions. He's speaking now. Five minutes on, the secretary returns with some documents. The client apologizes to you again as he studies various bits of paper. He seems disturbed by something he is reading; pensively, he picks up his pen, signs the cheque and hands it over. The secretary leaves the room.

- You now realize that there is a breakdown of attention here. The client's definitely not with it now. It's certainly not furthering your cause. You're wasting your breath. You can barely remember what you've said; what hope for him? However, you carry on. Somebody enters with two cups of coffee.

- Halfway through your preamble, your client's phone rings. More apologies. It's his boss wanting some figures for the departmental meeting in 15 minutes' time. He puts down the phone and starts fumbling through his in-tray.

- 'Do carry on talking,' he says to you, as he flicks through sheets of paper, searching for the required report. He doesn't find it. He looks defeated. 'I'm sorry. One of those days. Keep talking. But could I ask you to be brief?'

Brief?!

This is a frustrating scenario, but quite a common one. Most of us have experienced it (*or have subjected somebody to something similar*) during a job interview, a meeting with the boss to discuss something important to you (or to the boss), a meeting with a client, during a sales presentation. This scenario knows no bounds!

The point: **it's difficult to control attention when there isn't any in the first place**.

This example highlights what happens in varying degrees in many meetings and interviews. There is a breakdown of attention, which is totally beyond our control.

It would be better, at the point of being asked to be brief, to call a halt to the proceedings (depending on the circumstances, of course). You could suggest returning at another time, when the other person is less likely to be distracted and/or under time pressure.

To continue under such unfavourable circumstances is a waste of time and effort; the other person's mind is elsewhere. A hurried discussion is fair to neither party. Try the suggestion of making another appointment. The inconvenience involved may not seem worthwhile, but if you're determined to get a 'message' through then it's preferable. Also, you've helped the other person out of a tight spot. The next time you should at least receive more sympathetic attention.

Keeping the audience's attention or interest is probably the bedrock of any successful conversation or meeting. Everything else follows from that.

> **No attention = no communication = no result**

But most people fail to recognize when somebody's attention is wavering. It's up to you to pick up the signals and act accordingly.

The problem is this: when presenting an idea, demand, request, sales pitch or whatever, it's usually crucial to get the point across at the first attempt – assuming conditions are conducive. This initial discussion usually shapes the eventual outcome. Having rejected an idea in the *first* instance, most people do not like to change their minds later – even if they know they're wrong. It's sometimes a question of pride. They may not want to look indecisive or as though they were incapable of making the right evaluation in the first place.

Suppose you're making a pitch for something. Who wants to waste a good presentation (and, more importantly, time) on somebody whose mind is simply not there? If your proposal is only half heard, then your chances of success are reduced by 50 per cent immediately. So, if you want somebody to buy your product, to agree to your request for next Thursday off, to accept your proposal of marriage or to understand your reasons for handing in your resignation, you need their full attention. Otherwise, it's better to try to defer the conversation. Remember: **you usually get only one chance**.

The numerous interruptions experienced in the situation just described can be analysed to show the possible effect on the client's receptiveness; in other words, how the disturbances affect his attention span.

1 In the first three minutes your client absorbs *most* of what you say.

2 The telephone rings. His mind is now on the *subject of the telephone conversation* (the advertising agency wants to know whether to amend the copy for the new advertisement: could he call them back by 3 p.m?). He puts down the phone when he's finished the call.

3 You go on talking and he nods repeatedly (*thinking to himself*, while 'listening', 'Mmm, maybe we should have spot colour for the logo on this new ad . . .').

4 His secretary brings a cheque to be signed. He's not satisfied and asks her to return with some supporting documents.

5 You resume where you left off – *you can just about remember this yourself* – and he listens. (*But he's thinking*: 'How could the cheque be for that much? They must have made an addition error on their invoice. I'll ask Joanna to . . . I know, I bet they're trying to sting us for . . .')

6 You ask him a question relating to the Internet software, but he's not prepared; he's on the wrong track. *That's because he's missed most of what has been said.*

7 The secretary returns with some documents. He reluctantly signs the cheque.

8 You begin to talk – but now you can almost *see* the client's 'wheels' turning ('I should have queried that invoice with the suppliers; their bills never show a meaningful breakdown. Our financial director's really going to give me a hard time at the departmental meeting . . .'). But all the time he's nodding away in acknowledgement of what's being said.

How deceptive. But it's up to you to look for the signs. You can tell by the person's eyes and their expression whether their mind is elsewhere. **If you know you've lost their attention, it's better to stop**.

The attention curve

Audience attention is best represented as a curve. Maintaining a steady rise is virtually impossible. The ideal curve would be very hard or impossible for anyone to attain (see Figure 3.1).

The curves are more likely to be formed with intermittent waves: attention is gained, falls away and is then built up again (see Figure 3.2).

Fact: **people are always losing the thread of a conversation** (we're all human!) and need something explained again. But they won't admit it. There are numerous reasons for this:

- They don't want to seem impolite.
- They don't want to look stupid.
- They feel guilty for letting their minds wander (in other words, for 'two-timing' you).
- They have decided they're not interested and they 'switch off'.
- They don't want to prolong a conversation because they have another engagement lined up; or they've just got a lot to do.

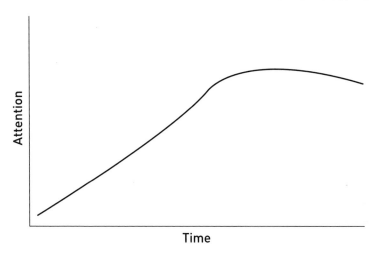

Figure 3.1 Ideal attention curve: attention is held and maintained from the start

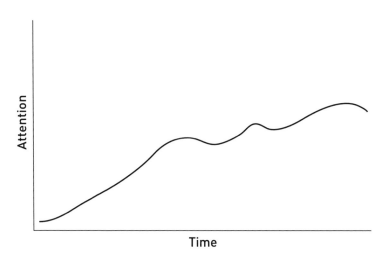

Figure 3.2 Typical attention curve, with intermittent waves

If this happens to you, it's your responsibility to take corrective action to try to regain the person's attention.

Programme your mind to retain an attention curve, to be applied in any meeting situation. This will allow you to *visualize* the peaks and troughs in your dialogue. You'll be able to evaluate lapses of concentration that much better by seeing an imaginary curve with highs and lows. You may find it difficult at first, but after trying this out in appropriate situations you'll discover how invaluable it is.

When you see a trough happening, you should try to find out why. Are you being boring? Or have they missed a main point? Or were you speaking in jargon? Because we can't see another person's mind engaging in 'two-timing', we have to look for the give-away signals, or be alert and understand enough to notice when concentration lapses.

You should be aware of the different types of distractions that can cause loss of concentration:

- Your listener **disagrees** with something you've said (and starts thinking about it).
- **Visual** distractions.
- Constant **interruptions** from other people.

Listener disagrees

Somebody who disagrees with something you've said may go off at a tangent in their own mind and lose the thread of what you're saying:

'Of course, I think he's too inexperienced to make a good prime minister. The other fella . . . Well, I know he's got his . . .' (*Listener disagrees and their concentration lapses.*)

'Well, you had the opportunity to make your feelings known before you started dating him. You see, when I was your age our mothers told us . . .' (*Listener disagrees.*)

'I have to say, Mr Mills, I think you'll find that quick, responsive service facilities should be of more concern to you than durability . . .' (*Listener disagrees.*)

In some cases, if you've said something that your listener disagrees with strongly, the listener may just be waiting for the earliest opportunity to end a meeting. Anything you say is wasted.

Visual distractions

A visual distraction is anything that triggers our overactive minds, forcing us to blot out a 'message' coming across to us:

- You're watching *Hamlet* at the theatre and you notice that Ophelia is wearing a watch. The distraction is so great for a few minutes that you miss the dialogue and artistry.

- You're with a prospective client in a restaurant; he suddenly spots somebody he knows seated in the far corner. He constantly looks away to see whether that person has noticed him; you can see his attention wavering.

- If you're talking to somebody who has a stain on their jacket, or a prominent button missing with the loose thread hanging, that can be enough to distract your mind from following the gist of any conversation.

So, if, for example, you rip your sleeve on the reception filing cabinet coming in, or lose a vital button in the car park and are aware that you look untidy, tell the other person. Their knowing that you know should be enough to stop them wondering about the offending flaw. Case closed.

Equally, if there's to be a meeting in your office and there are potential visual distractions there, try to anticipate them. Turn the photos the other way round!

I'm reminded of a true case recounted to me many years ago by a work colleague. Going to see a prominent advertising agency, he was greeted by warm smiles as he waited in reception; even those people leaving the building smiled at him warmly. He was impressed with the friendliness of the company. When he was shown into the office of the account director he was seeing, the whole meeting was punctuated with further warm smiles, from all those present. He left the office, thinking to himself how well the meeting had gone – they were all so friendly, full of smiles.

Even the taxi driver who took him back to his own company's offices was smiling the whole time. When he got back to work, popping in to the WC first, he glanced in the mirror to comb his hair; on his face, to his horror, he noticed four small bits of blue toilet tissue that he had stuck over his cuts after shaving that morning. I know – you're dying to ask – did he get the business from the advertising agency? No. They didn't hear a word he said!

Dealing with constant interruptions

It's annoying when you're having a conversation with some-body and you're constantly interrupted. You're in a restaurant with a friend, excitedly telling her about the new job you've just got, and the waiter keeps coming and interrupting you, even though you've said you'll let him know when you're ready for coffee. You're giving a colleague at work some instructions on how to operate a complicated system and a junior clerk repeat-edly interrupts you, asking unimportant questions.

In the workplace, it's unproductive when you're with a boss, colleague or client if your conversation is continually disturbed. The attention curve for the earlier example that we analysed is shown in Figure 3.3.

But as the working environment becomes increasingly pres-surized, the above scenarios are all too common. With people taking on more and more, 'downsizing', open-plan offices, etc., few meetings are completely free from interruptions. You have to live with it. Unfortunately, the onus is usually on you (with a message to impart or an idea to sell) *to detect a breakdown of attention* and carry out the salvage operation.

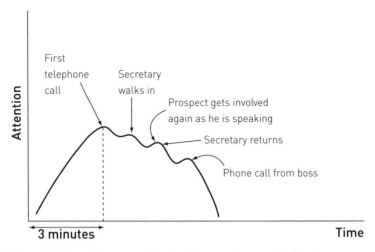

Figure 3.3 Attention curve, showing interruptions and their effects

If the disruption is in **human** form, you can at least categorize the nature of any problem involved because you hear what is said. You can then evaluate its possible effect on your listener's concentration.

With a **telephone** distraction, you have to try to observe the other person's facial expressions and check the tone of voice if the conversation turns monosyllabic. The reason could be, for example:

● Their boss calling to give them a dressing down.

● Their partner announcing they're leaving.

● Their secretary informing them that their car has just been clamped.

● An irate client threatening to cancel a sizeable contract.

● Their son phoning to say he's dropping out of university.

● The production department telling them that delivery for a major client will not go out on time as originally promised.

Unless they refer to the phone call, you'll have to guess the likely level of distraction from their eyes and tone of voice. If they look mildly or seriously preoccupied, what is the answer?

Repeat. I repeat: *repeat*. **Give the person a summary of what you said** *before* the interruption.

People are always concerned about sounding parrot-like in their discussions. But consider this: **research shows continually that people take in only about 40 per cent of what they hear.** (And that's *without* interruptions.)

So, by recapping you increase your chances of making your point stick.

After an interruption, visualize the mental **attention curve** and pick up on the points made *before* you were silenced. You can do this briefly. The other person's new problem has blotted out part of what you said earlier, so you're helping them to come back into the discussion. You're into their mind and working out where the breakdowns have occurred. Rescue the discussion – and save the situation.

By summarizing what you've said each time, you're also helping the other person to crystallize all the benefits that you've been discussing. In the case of a job interview, for example, all may not be lost as you encapsulate to the interviewer your worthy achievements and capabilities. If you're there making a sales pitch, you're doing the same thing: restating the benefits that you referred to earlier. Besides, by being able to extract the salient points of your presentation, you're showing that your line of thinking is logical and structured. It enhances your stature.

It's impossible to get totally undivided attention as long as the other person is capable of engaging in stray thoughts (this applies to all of us). It does help, though, to recognize how **supplementary thoughts caused by interruptions and distractions can defocus your own presentation**. If you know how to recognize it, you can at least do something about it.

Ways to win more attention

Change the seating if possible

This principle applies everywhere, but let's take the workplace setting as an example, where a desk quite often separates the sender and receiver of a message. The person whose desk it is cannot get away (mentally or physically) from the piled-up proof on his desk of all the work awaiting him.

So what? Anybody having a discussion from behind their desk is bound to be all too aware of the paperwork waiting there to be done. You know from your own experience: it's there in front of you, reminding you of how busy you are. ('In fact, I'm so busy, what the hell am I doing talking to this person?') This allows all sorts of random thoughts to enter the head: *'Mmm, I must remember to write a reply to that letter. Oh, I must get that out by Friday. What's that green bit of paper there? Oh no, I forgot to renew that subscription . . . Hey, Fran's spelt "analysis" wrong in that email.'*

It's a consequence of being on your own territory. You can see your workload grow in front of your eyes, bringing distraction with it. A vague anxiety sets in. It's not fair on the other person.

You should be aware of this territorial problem. If you've experienced the desk-bound type before, **you would be wise to try to get them out of the hot seat to a calmer corner of the room** – in other words, away from the desk. Take the lead in changing the scene.

Avoid breaks

Awareness of the attention curve reminds you that the best possible situation is to sustain attention on that upward curve as far as you can. Given that we decide on most things on an **emotional** basis, it follows that *timing* is all important to catch the fleeting emotion that says: 'Yes, I'm happy to offer you the job' or 'Tell me more' or 'OK, we'll try out your product – we'll give it a go' or 'Yes, you can have the day off on Wednesday.' Anything that lowers that momentary emotional high can turn a decision the other way.

So it's up to you to keep the other person's attention on that incline and not to break the spell.

Imagine you've been watching a film on TV for the past 45 minutes. The car is now twelve feet from the edge of the cliff and the handbrake cable snaps; it's rolling down towards the edge! Click, click: commercial break.

When the film resumes after three minutes, do you still have the same feeling? That feeling of sustained drama that had you concentrating intently for three-quarters of an hour? The suspension of disbelief that had completely engrossed you and stopped your own mind wandering for the duration of the film? The short answer to these questions is 'No'. The break has forced you to lose that state of high emotion. The spell is broken.

It's no different in interpersonal situations. You've been discussing a possible promotional campaign with a managing director for half an hour or so. She's quite interested, it appears.

'Have you got some more case studies you can show me?' she asks.

'Yes, I'll just dig them out from my case.'

You pick up your case and start to search. As it's taking such a long time, the MD turns to check her emails. She has the courtesy to look up three minutes later, but as you're still searching frantically she carries on attending to her own work.

'Ah, this is it – no, that's . . . Wait, I think this is a good example. No, sorry. I've got it here somewhere.'

Of course, eye contact has been lost for some time now. You've been too busy on a paper chase. The MD's emotional state has shifted now. Her acceptance level is starting to slip, as well as her confidence in you. Her thoughts are now turning to the letters she has to sign, where she's meeting her friend for lunch and why she shouldn't proceed with your proposition.

Eventually, the sheets of paper are located.

'Let me see now. There were three concurrent campaigns in different regions in this example. The costs are calculated differently in this case . . .'

Out comes the calculator: more lost eye contact.

'Well, that doesn't seem right. Maybe I pressed the minus instead of . . . No, I couldn't . . . I wonder if the battery . . . ?'

Two to three minutes of calculator malfunction follow. Nothing is as boring as watching people tap away at calculator keys (second only to watching paint dry), especially when you don't have confidence in their dexterity.

By now, our bored decision-maker has lost that 'high' and has all but come down to earth with a bump. This is not an unusual situation. It happens all the time.

It's important to analyse the situation. It's not that the potential client doesn't think the proposition is a good one. *It's just that the feeling of wanting to go ahead has gone*. She'll 'think about it' and perhaps pursue it in the future, but avoid a gamble at the present time.

The lesson? Recognize that most decisions of acceptance – for anything – are made on an **emotional** level. It is important to get acceptance when **feeling** is running high.

So avoid interrupting your discussion or presentation by taking your eyes away from the other person. If you do that, you give them licence to 'stray'. Have your props at hand. If you need to use a calculator, do it slickly.

The attention curve for this example would look something like that in Figure 3.4.

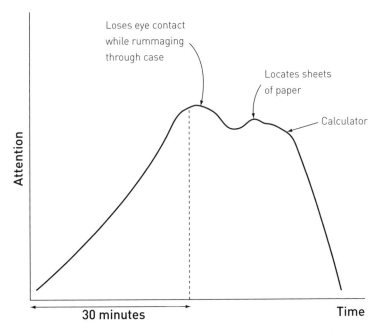

Loses eye contact
while rummaging
through case

Locates sheets
of paper

Calculator

Attention

30 minutes

Time

Figure 3.4 Example attention curve: for 30 minutes there is good attention; then attention falls sharply

Say what you're going to say

We can perhaps call this the golden rule for holding attention and making your message memorable and understood. Say what you're going to say. Say it. Say what you said.

First, you're telling your audience what you will be speaking about. If it's a subject of interest (and, of course, you would make sure it is), it keeps people interested. Then you actually tell them about it. Finally, you recap on what you've actually said.

On the basis that most people take in only about **40 per cent** of what they hear, this formula increases our chances of being heard (Figure 3.5).

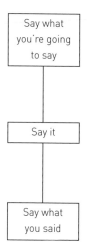

Figure 3.5 The golden rule for holding attention

Coffee break . . .

Attention is held only when interest is r_____; other-wise people start listening to themselves – so keep them interested.

Since people are constantly 'running their own tapes' in their heads, it's up to you to spot when a b_____ of attention occurs.

People don't usually a_____ when they've lost the thread of a conversation.

Your mental 'attention curve' is invaluable in allowing you to visualize a lapse of c_____ – and how best to deal with it.

Distractions that threaten the momentum of a conversa-tion can be threefold:

– a disagreement or some confusion about what has been s_____;
– v_____ distractions;
– i_____ from another person.

Most decisions of acceptance are made on an e_____ level when feelings are running high – so don't 'neglect' the other person by losing too much eye contact in favour of dealing with papers and props.

Remember at all times: people take in only about _____ per cent of what they hear (and that's without interruptions).

Try to avoid (during your discussion) taking your e_____ away from the other person, for any length of time.

Chapter

'The average person looks without seeing, listens without hearing, touches without feeling, eats without tasting, moves without physical awareness ... and talks without thinking.'

Leonardo da Vinci

Mind your body language

How to read non-verbal signals from others and send out the right ones

- Why is 'non-verbal' important?
- If life is like a game of cards ...
- Using empathy to pick up signs of body language
- Smile, and the whole world ...
- Body-language gestures
- Avoiding negative body-language signals
- Other gestures
- Spatial relationships

Of course, communication is more than just speaking and listening. We also express feelings in a non-verbal fashion when we're engaging in both of these activities: truly effective communicators can both *read* and *use* non-verbal language to increase their impact and ability to persuade.

We want to understand better the people that we interact with. After all, you know from your own 'performances' that what you say is often very different from what you think or feel.

1 You talk to somebody and you're 'sending' a message to them both verbally and non-verbally (in scientific terms you are known as the **encoder**).

2 They 'receive' the message, *interpret* it in a certain way and send back to you a message that is both verbal and non-verbal (the **decoder**).

3 You respond to their reply in a verbal and non-verbal way.

The encoder sends behaviours to be interpreted and the decoder receives the behaviours and interprets them according to their *own* parameters. (Sounds like trouble brewing!) And, of course, we're constantly changing our 'roles' as either encoder or decoder as we take our turn to assume either a speaking role or a listening role.

The problem in our interactions with other people is that there are two forms of behavioural messages that we give out. The first is what non-verbal experts Ekman and Friesen (1969) call an 'informative act', which results in certain interpretations on the part of the receiver that actually do not have any active or conscious intent on the part of the sender. So a person's non-verbal behaviour is **unintentionally** 'giving off' signals that can be correctly or incorrectly interpreted by a decoder. The second form of message has been called the 'communicative act', where the encoder **intentionally** attempts to send a specific message to the receiver.

The process continues. We're all at it! In fact, the work done by psychologists over the years continually puts an average figure of around **40–45 per cent for the verbal part of our message** (which includes the way the words are said – what's termed *paralanguage*) and **55–60 per cent for visual body language** in a typical face-to-face conversation with another person. In other words, only about half of a meaning comes from the words and the way they are said; the other half emanates from the speaker's visual non-verbal messages. Because so many of our daily interactions revolve around speech, it's small wonder that we forget that it forms a small percentage of our everyday communication.

What does this tell us? It indicates clearly that for optimum interpersonal success, we need to be more aware of non-verbal behaviour rather than just listening to the words used. That is to say, that we judge actions quite separately from speech as a guide to a person's inner feelings.

The impression you make and the impressions you receive are influenced greatly by your non-verbal behaviours.

We can note three main purposes of body language:

- When it's used *instead* of speech.
- When it's used to *reinforce* speech.
- When it displays (or betrays) a person's *mood*.

When it comes to meeting people for the first time, the research carried out by social psychologists emphasizes the importance of *first impressions* and the impact that is made in the first few minutes. This applies to both our social and our professional lives. We take in all aspects of a person's appearance, from their personal characteristics to their clothes and body language. Of course, this is hardly error-free. Rather, it should alert us to what occurs in everyday life, what we should do when we observe and also what happens when we ourselves are the subject of observation.

The important thing is that it's all about **perception**. I'll digress with a little joke for a moment:

> An old man dies and goes to Hell. When he gets there, he sees his friend, a 95-year-old 'decrepit' man, with a beautiful woman sitting on his knee. He says to his friend: *'This can't be Hell, you're not being punished, you're having fun,'* to which his friend replies: *'This is punishment – for her!'*

What this highlights is a key element about thought. What the joke displays is a switch in **perception**. This is important in changing the way we think and consequently the way we 'read' a situation.

Studies (carried out by Edward de Bono) have shown that 90 per cent of error in thinking is due to error in perception. **If you can change your perception, you can change your emotion and this leads to new ideas and insights**.

Non-verbal behaviour *outside* business and the workplace is easier to read than that which is typically displayed in the working world. Here there is more 'masking' as **people take on different roles and often have to suppress their true feelings.** Mastery of the reading of signals in a working environment is an excellent foundation for your social life, as the principles are essentially the same. In every encounter with another human being, our moods and emotions at that point in time are exhibited (for potential analysis) to discerning others: they can be perceived in the posture, position and movement of our bodies. Nobody can be expected to share our subjective inner thoughts. They are, after all, private property. And yet we are able to pick up various emotions in others and can communicate our feelings to them: the traffic is two-way if both parties are empathetic.

The term 'body language' is often used to describe our non-verbal behaviour. Its role in interpersonal communication is of paramount importance. Without saying a single word, you are conveying an impression with your own body language.

> **You cannot *not* communicate.**

Why is 'non-verbal' important?

♫ If you could read my mind ...
  what a tale my thoughts could tell ... ♫

As the song reminds us, if we could only read people's minds what thoughts might we receive – and how at odds might those thoughts be compared with what the person had just uttered to us (their words)!

'That was a great party.' (Mind-reading: I wish I'd stayed in and watched the *X Factor*.)

'Yes, well thank you for coming in today. You'll hear from us within a week – we have some other people to interview.' (Mind-reading: Just go, please – wasting my time . . . he's got to be kidding. How does he expect me to understand the jargon used in his current firm – you'd think my quizzical look would have alerted him . . .)

'No, of course I don't mind you borrowing the lawnmower again.' (Mind-reading: They're turning out to be the neighbours from hell. Damn nerve. That's the fifth time she's borrowed it – she said a year ago they were about to buy one.)

Well, perhaps it's better that we can't read minds because it would be two-way traffic; the other person would be reading *our* thoughts too. Anyhow, if we can't read minds as such, we do need to be able to 'read' people to try to discern the unspoken. We have to read their body language to gain an insight into what's going on in their mind. Remember, their mind and body are one.

It is this non-verbal aspect of communication that provides us with the best clues as to a person's true feelings. To be successful at 'reading' body language, it is essential to piece together elements of a person's behaviour as a kind of jigsaw and to look at the behaviours in context, *not in isolation*. After all, body language is not a science, but as you learn to observe different gestures, mannerisms and paralanguage you become more adept at it, as with any other skill that you acquire.

Just a word of caution. You read magazines and books telling you in a definite way that a certain gesture indicates this, another one that. First of all, you have to look for 'clusters' of information that may support your evaluation. Second, it's not infallible.

However, in the absence of genuine 'mind-reading' it will give you a better insight into what's going on in the other person's mind.

Usually, when people try to conceal their feelings, they have to work exceptionally hard at their non-verbal display. It's much harder than controlling verbal output (although paralanguage give-aways – see below – are often present), but even the facade of appropriate words may be betrayed by emotional **'leakage'**, which is difficult to control.

More and more focus is now given to understanding another person's emotions in order to communicate successfully with them, and in instances where we are trying to 'get on the same wavelength' to move them from point A to point B. Body language is the primary method of communicating emotions to another person, and so being able to read it effectively and display empathy back to the other person is paramount.

Back in the 1960s, Dr Albert Mehrabian, a professor at University College of Los Angeles, provided us with some fascinating research which is continually cited whenever the subject of body language is discussed. He gave us the well-worn digits: 55, 38 and 7, noticing that most individuals were guilty of sending mixed messages. He found that the impact of a message could be classified as **55 per cent visual (non-verbal), 38 per cent vocal (such things as tone of voice, rhythm, inflection) and 7 per cent verbal (meaning the actual words used)**.

So, in a face-to-face encounter:

- 93 per cent of the impact of your message is **non-verbal** (55 per cent what you *see*, 38 per cent on how it *sounds*).
- 7 per cent of the impact of your message is **verbal** (the words: *what* and how you *say* them).

More than 50 years later this study is still cited for illumination – *and sometimes with scepticism*. Why scepticism? Well, only from those people who challenge the way the study was carried out. Yet Mehrabian's emphasis was not on the precision of the 55/38/7 split, but on the 'weighting' of the importance of non-verbal and verbal communication.

Successive studies over the decades have confirmed the validity of this research. Although there is an inevitable slight variation in the figures, all agree that the **visual** accounts for more than half of our interpretation of feelings and attitudes, with **sound** being the second factor, followed by the actual content – the **words** spoken.

Put simply, this tells us that most of the messages in any interaction with another person (face to face) are revealed through body signals or 'bodytalk'.

If we analyse the function of language in our everyday interpersonal situations, its purpose is to convey our ideas, our thoughts and our feelings; if it does this adequately then we have communicated well. This does not have to occur *solely* by the use of our words. Even with our words, a lot depends on our delivery, as we see below.

Paralanguage

As outlined above, if we take the results of the study, of the 93 per cent non-verbal communication 55 per cent is **body language** and 38 per cent relates to non-verbal aspects of **speech**.

These non-verbal aspects of speech are termed '**paralinguistics**' – they relate to the tone of voice and related cues; in other words, the vocal changes or variations in the voice. It is important to look at this interesting area of paralinguistics since it forms such a high percentage of communication. It relates to:

- *Volume*: loudness or softness will depend on what we are trying to convey. We may add emphasis to words by speaking more loudly (or the opposite).
- *Rate of speaking*: this can affect the amount of understanding the audience receives. For example, somebody who speaks

really fast may lose the listener's attention. Equally, a slow speaker can make the audience lose interest.

● *Tone, pitch and inflection*: a person's pitch can go from low to high. In the course of everyday conversations, we'll adjust our pitch and alter our inflection. For example, you'll observe that a lot of people have a rising pitch when they're asking a question. Skilful use of tone, pitch and inflection can enhance your message positively. Remember what you are conveying through natural variation. See how changes in emphasis affect these identical statements – does each convey the same meaning?

 – You want me to go?

 – You want *me* to go!

 – *You* want *me* to go!

We said earlier that body language plays a great role in supporting our words; paralanguage plays an equally important part, whether it's adding a negative or a positive slant to our words. It gives words meaning and makes for a more effective speaker.

Mixed messages and the 'higher figure'

So this 38 per cent of communication is concerned with how a person **sounds** when conversing with you – and equally the impression you give when you are talking to a person. Non-verbal behaviour is always two-way traffic. Your sound is a reflection of your **emotional** state.

The other 7 per cent – the words – **are no less important**. They just assume a **lower** priority if the other elements are not right. Just a particular word or phrase can completely alter the communication chain (see Chapter 6).

Perhaps the most important finding of this research is the effect on our interpretations whenever there's a **mixed message** between the three elements. In other words: when what you **hear** *conflicts* with what you **see** (and vice-versa of course). The research concluded that in a mixed-message situation we'll believe the **higher figure** (as the true interpretation).

You know this from your own real-life situations:

Natasha (to husband, absorbed in the *Financial Times* share prices):
'Can I just show you this swatch for the curtains for the back bedroom.
I know they're a bit expensive but . . . have you got a minute?'

Husband (looks up from the newspaper, takes off glasses and puts
calculator and pen aside): 'Yeah, OK. Go on then.' (Impatient tone
of voice.)

There's a mixed message here. The words are saying 'Yes' but the tone is saying something else. What would you believe to be the true meaning of the message? The *words* or the *way* the words are said?

More than likely, it's the husband's *tone* that is revealing his true feelings – the higher figure, the 38 per cent. Remember – we'll always believe the **higher** figure: in this case the tone rather than the words (7 per cent). Natasha would be better off – if she's astute enough to pick up the emotions leaking out through his tone – saying to her husband that, on reflection, she'll talk to him later. She may get less resistance (depending on what he's read about share prices in the *FT*!).

If life is like a game of cards . . .

. . . then dealing with people is like a game of poker. That's because poker is all about how good you are with people skills. It's being intuitive enough to be able to read the other players' body language and at the same time being able to 'mask' your own feelings so that they can't 'read' you. In the game of poker you'll hear the term 'tell', which refers to a player's body language give-away.

In real life we often need to keep our emotions in check. It may be deliberate on your part – to give a certain impression – or it may be just the way you are. Much of our body language is learned and then turns into habit over the years. **But the important thing to consider is this: is it working for you or against you?**

Sarah: 'So I really don't know whether to splash out on the Aga in case the sale falls through.'

Jane (chin resting on right hand, rubbing eyes repeatedly): 'Yes. I know.'

Sarah: 'I mean, look what happened to Liz in HR after she had her offer accepted . . . I mean . . .'

Jane (staring to the side and then looking down at her coffee cup): 'Well, I know.'

Sarah's thinking: 'Jane's not interested in my problems. She's jealous because I'm getting a new house and she's stuck in her two-bedroom flat.' It could just be that Jane had lost sleep the night before for some reason and was not feeling too good, and so displayed body-language signs of lack of attentiveness. If that's the case, there has been a misinterpretation of the message. With damaging consequences.

It's so important to be aware of how you may appear to others because body language – being 'silent' in its delivery – does not elicit a reply if the message has been interpreted wrongly. In the above example, Jane did not mean to give an impression of inattention but Sarah received this silent message. Another scenario:

Mr Pearson: 'Do sit down, Mr Caine. You've brought the files with you, I take it?'

Mr Caine: 'Yes, I've got them here.' (Sits down, looks at watch pointedly, looks up at Mr Pearson, then stares at his own shoe at the end of his tapping foot.)

Mr Pearson: 'I felt that if we just went through the figures together, we could agree on how we can change the budgets next year so that nobody loses out in significant terms.' (Leans forward slightly and maintains eye contact with a smile.)

Mr Caine: 'That's OK by me.'

Mr Pearson: 'I've got a simplistic breakdown here. If we take just one person from your department we'll cut down on the salaries budget by enough to take space at the exhibitions in Boston and the new one over in the Channel Islands in Guernsey. What do you think?'

Mr Caine: 'If that's what we have to do, so be it.' (Starts to pull fluff off his jacket, graduating down to his trousers.)

Mr Pearson: 'But how do you really feel about this. Tell me, because it has got to be a joint decision. I may even bring Mr Henson in on this.'

Mr Caine: 'Fine by me. I take it you don't mean whoever goes has to go immediately?' (Continues searching for fluff and has now reached his left sock.)

At this point, Mr Pearson politely makes up an excuse to terminate the meeting under the pretext of having just remembered that he had to get something done for head office. Everything about Mr Caine's body language had shown disagreement. And Mr Pearson showed enough perspicacity to pick up the signals.

There could have been a reason for Mr Caine's mood that day, or there may have been a more important underlying reason for his disapproval. Either way, it would probably have been unwise to continue the meeting in the hope of a productive outcome. The two individuals could at least go away and think about it and possibly seek third-party advice, or whatever. Mr Pearson could make enquiries to try to find out any hidden concerns on the part of Mr Caine.

Using empathy to pick up signs of body language

So, it is imperative that if we're to be effective in interpersonal communication in our personal and work life, we should be as concerned with our non-verbal cues as with our verbal ones. **Feelings are displayed better by non-verbal messages**. The outward signs of people's internal emotional states are their facial expressions, body movements and gestures, postures, vocal clues and other behaviours.

Facial expressions obviously do much to communicate feelings. It is the face and the eyes that are the most revealing in terms of non-verbal behaviour. We interpret other people's emotions and their attitudes towards us initially from their facial expressions.

We tend to trust people much more if their facial expressions are congruent with (i.e. match) the words coming out of their mouth. We're influenced more by people who display this than by people whose actions are incongruent.

How can people trust the passion and enthusiasm of a speaker if their face displays tension and uncertainty and is unsmiling?

Research shows that there is a universal recognition of several facial expressions. We are quite successful at recognizing six different emotions that are displayed on the human face:

- sadness
- surprise
- disgust
- anger
- happiness
- fear.

The fact that the expression of these emotions has proved to be universal, spanning the whole cultural spectrum, has led to the conclusion that it is inborn rather than learned. However, it is relatively easy to regulate and control our facial expressions. In body language terms, the face is the most expressive part of us and indicates our thoughts, feelings and moods.

A lot can be said with the face. We use facial expressions in everyday life to communicate feelings to other people. If someone says something we disagree with, or we believe they're telling a lie, or if they've said something that's embarrassing to another person then without saying a single word we can give a 'look' that conveys our message to them. Norma Desmond's song in the musical *Sunset Boulevard* puts it well:

♫ **... With one look, I put words to shame ...**
With one look you'll know all you need to know ... ♫

We also use our faces to reinforce a verbal message that we may be giving. But we have to be cautious. We often hear the expression: 'It's written all over your face'; but we know how easy it is to conceal our true feelings. Have you ever watched the losing nominees at the Oscars applaud the winner as they clutch the trophy? If we make our judgements based *only* on facial expression, we can be extremely inaccurate in judging emotions.

Observation shows that human beings physically mimic the actions of others in certain situations to convey understanding. In particular, we may mimic distress when another person is exhibiting that emotion; it is basically an expression of sympathy to that person.

Smile, and the whole world . . .

Of all the facial expressions we are capable of transmitting, it is accepted that the one that needs to be encouraged is the smile. Happiness is the only **positive** emotion we can show through the face. People aren't good at giving genuine smiles. There seems to be a problem with getting eyes and mouth in harmony. If you smile with just your mouth and not your eyes it gives that 'snarling' look. (Seen it before? I bet you have!)

What are we trying to convey in most of our interpersonal dealings with other people: a negative or a positive state? Do we feel better when we're in a negative state or a positive state? You know how it is. You're in a good mood and you come across somebody who (for no valid reason) is miserable and unsmiling. *Doesn't it take away some of your joy?* There seems to be only one answer: **smile**. It will cost you nothing and will leave behind you a trail of goodwill.

Plus there are a whole host of physiological benefits too, such as an increase of blood flow to the brain, which improves our mood. Research has shown that the forcing of a particular expression on your face causes the mind and body to respond.

Biochemical changes take place and the hormones make you feel better and more positive. **Feeling more positive helps to achieve more positive outcomes**. The groundbreaking research taught us that the opposite of what was commonly perceived is actually true: that emotions can *follow* facial expressions as opposed to always *preceding* them.

So a person's facial expression actually does control emotions. And, of course, the act of smiling has an important effect on people you are dealing with, as it is proven time and time again (and it's something that you are probably well aware of, because you do it yourself) that people tend to mimic or 'mirror' the expressions of the other person. You'll also find you get to know people better and have better conversations with them, that your stress levels go down, you become more relaxed, people like you better, oh, and you inadvertently become more persuasive.

And just one other point – for both male and female readers – smiling involves just the one muscle whereas the other expressions require a lot of muscles to be contorted, here, there and everywhere.

Body-language gestures

You can exhibit a beaming smile when you're actually feeling quite morose. But what are difficult to control are our gestures and our tone of voice (which we shall look at later).

Eye contact

Eye contact is a particularly effective non-verbal means of establishing good interpersonal communication. When we look at someone, they are aware that they have our attention. It then directs the course of the interchange, so its importance cannot be overstressed. We tend to use eye contact for feedback purposes, to make the speaker aware that we are listening to them. We in turn need a signal that they know we are listening to them.

We tend to use eye contact automatically and unconsciously, and perhaps not enough in many work instances. Think about yourself in your work life. How much eye contact do you do? Think about your work colleagues. How do they compare with you? We tend to engage in more eye contact when we're in a listening situation. A speaker should look at their audience – of one or one hundred – to obtain feedback. If you don't look, you won't know:

- whether they're still with you;
- whether they understand what you're saying;
- whether you're proceeding too rapidly for comprehension; and, of course,
- whether they agree.

Lack of eye contact gives the impression that you are talking *at* people instead of *to* them.

There has been research to suggest that when talking to people, if they look to the left they are searching their memory for 'stored' knowledge; if they look to the right then they're using their imagination. It can be an imperceptible flicker sometimes, almost in the 'blink of an eye' (literally!).

Increasing eye contact generally has a positive effect. It can show that you're attentive, that you like somebody and that you're sincere; it can initiate a communication between two people and maintain the interchange once a dialogue has started; it can be a tremendous 'influencer' when trying to persuade somebody to buy your point of view or product; and, on the basis that we fix and maintain eye contact with somebody we're attracted to, it's good for romance.

Use of gestures

When most people talk of body language, they are referring **to the use of gestures that provide added meaning**. Research by psychologists over the years has shown that these gestures typically can be split into five categories:

- *Emblems*: these are particular movement(s) used instead of words – non-verbal acts that have a meaning that can easily be understood and can originate in any area of the body. The more obvious examples are facial expressions such as frowning, or hand movements such as giving a thumbs-up signal. Care has to be taken with different cultures as 'unintentional' communication can occur when encoder and decoder interpret completely different meanings from the emblematic display.

- *Illustrators*: movement(s) used along with speech to illustrate what has been verbalized.

- *Regulators*: movements related to our function of speaking or listening, indicating our intentions. For example, head nods, eye contact, shifts of body position.

- *Adaptors*: movements, such as drumming the fingers, pulling hair or fiddling with an item of jewellery, that indicate emotions. In other words, behavioural habits. They can be classified into three types:

  (a) *self*-adaptors, such as smoothing down the hair, scratching the head or steepling the fingers;

  (b) *alter*-adaptors, which would include arm-folding or protective hand movements to represent intimacy, withdrawal or flight;

  (c) *object*-adaptors, such as fiddling with an item of jewellery.

- *Affect displays*: clearer signals that reveal emotion, such as facial expressions. These are usually masked in social and work settings to display more acceptable behaviour.

If we're to make any sense of body language, it is essential that we don't take a gesture on its own, regardless of other gestures or the particular situation, and try to make an analysis. We should use the clues provided by a number of the speaker's gestures – known as '**cluster gestures**' – together with their verbal expressions. For example, in the meeting between the business colleagues described on p. 65, Mr Caine's staring at his shoe, looking at his watch, tapping his foot, picking fluff from his clothes and lack of real eye contact were a meaningful gesture cluster taken in conjunction with his unconvincing verbalizations.

The inconsistencies that occur between cues from different channels are known by psychologists as '**interchannel discrepancies**'.

If we receive from two separate channels of communication (i.e. verbal and non-verbal) a conflicting message, then the receiver will more likely believe *the message that is harder to fake*. This is usually the non-verbal message. Therefore, the non-verbal communication, rather than the verbal one, will be accepted as *true*. Whenever there's a mismatch between what we see and hear (i.e. it's not congruent – to use the jargon), we tend to believe the higher number.

So, for example, the content (words: the 7 per cent) may seem OK, but the emotional state of the person, as judged by their tone and faltering delivery (their paralanguage), suggests something is not quite right. Therefore, we'll believe the **higher** figure, the 38 per cent, as an indication of the trustworthiness of the message. So we're not persuaded that everything is as it seems.

For every human being, this is a situation that you've been exposed to frequently and one that you have exercised yourself. You've betrayed in your voice a tone that confuses the listener (your wife, partner, client, boss, relative, friend, customer) and sends a mixed message because it is impatient, defensive, abrasive, and so the listener (the decoder) 'receives' and therefore interprets – as we discussed earlier – something that you had not intended. Your 'leakage' has come out through your tone. The term 'leakage' is used in body-language terms to denote how the message you give someone verbally is *invalidated* by the truth leaking out visually (commonly from the lower half of the body). In other words, true emotions leak out even when a person tries to conceal them. If you are aware of your misdemeanour, it often helps the relationship if you – after you catch yourself in action – give an explanation to the person. For example, if you've had a bad morning: 'I've just had to fire our office manager – apologies if I sound impatient.'

- So words and paralanguage (**45 per cent**) may seem OK, but there may be shuffling in the chair, evasive eye contact, nervous tapping of the fingers, and this doesn't inspire trust. So we believe the **higher** figure, the **55 per cent**, as being the true indicator that we should use for our judgement. *We're not persuaded by the message.*

If it's you exhibiting this body language and there is a legitimate reason for it, then bring attention to the reason and there's a chance of salvaging some trust.

It is essential, if you want to successfully communicate the right message to your audience, that verbal and non-verbal messages are *congruent*. The two mustn't be at odds with each other. **Congruence and gesture clusters provide us with the means to interpret body language with a fair degree of accuracy.** As Carl Jung noted:

'The separation of psychology from the premises of biology is plainly artificial because the human psyche lives in indissoluble union with the body. The mind and body are one.'

Can you remember a time when you were sitting outside the interviewer's office acting calm and composed, smiling at the secretary – more creases in her sardonic face than in her dress – as she brings you a coffee, thinking: 'What does she know that I don't? Has somebody else already been given the job?'

You place the coffee cup on the table, sit up straight, adjust your clothes, cross your legs, uncross them, cross them again, fiddle with your watchstrap, smooth your hair, uncross your legs. By the time your prospective interrogator comes out to greet you – 'Good morning. We've been expecting you' – you're a nervous wreck!

'We've been expecting you Mr . . .'

Avoiding negative body-language signals

When we study body language and its effects, the most important thing to remember is that, regardless of what a particular gesture means to you, **it's how the receiver perceives it that's important**.

Various irritating body signals are commonly given out to others.

Crossed arms

There are a few variations to the arm-cross over the chest, but the message is the same. Usually it's a **defensive** stance; you'll see it on trains, in coffee bars, in lifts. It's usually associated with a brain that is signalling to you to be defensive. In a one-to-one or a meeting situation, you'll see it when the person *disagrees* with you, and consequently they don't pay *attention* to what you're saying. It should alert you to the fact that, unless you take action, you might as well give up. It would be pointless to continue even if they look as though they're agreeing with you by their communication of **verbal** behaviour. As we noted earlier, we believe the *higher* figure – the crossed arms negative body-language pose. There are some people who through habit or preference say that they feel more comfortable when they cross their arms over their chest. But, bearing in mind the situation with body language, it should always be remembered that you are taking in signals about the other person from their body language and at the same time giving out signals to the other person with your **non-verbals**.

The essential point here is that the 'leakage' signal can give you an opportunity to change tack before the other person has had a chance to put their feelings into words – *before it's too late*. It happens in family arguments, sales presentations, seminars, meetings with the boss and interviews. **One subtle method of getting the other person away from this 'closed' body position is to hand them something to look at**. Then try to get to the bottom of what it is they disagree with.

Anne (noticing that her nephew John has gone into the folded arms position after being ticked off – unfairly in his eyes – for once again forgetting her birthday; he'd had exams and was preoccupied): 'I kept this interesting cutting from last week's paper for Tanya about a memory system that has helped people in exams. Now, where did I put it? Oh, here it is. Have a look, John.' (Passes paper to John.)

John (unfolding his tight arm-cross): 'Yeah. Right. Thanks.'

Interviewee: 'Well, I don't really care for travelling that much, to be frank. I find it so disruptive when you get back from work trips. It takes me a while to readjust to life.'

Interviewer: 'So, if we picked up a client account with international offices, it's not an account that we could consider you for?' (Folds his arms and leans back. He's losing interest in this applicant, who at first seemed promising. True, the advertisement hadn't mentioned the need for overseas travel, but there was the chance that it might be necessary in the future.)

Interviewee (reading the body language and realizing he'd perhaps been a bit too frank): 'Oh, of course if a client account necessitated work with their overseas offices, it would be a challenge to work within the whole international corporate structure. It's not something I would want to pass up – far from it.'

Having verbally tried to allay the interviewer's concerns, the interviewee now wants to create an open body position on the other side of the desk, so he says: 'Could I just show you this artwork from . . . ?'

Interviewer: 'Sure.' (Reaches over to accept it.)

Back to open body position!

Sitting positions

We can often deduce a person's mindset from the way they are sitting:

- Leg-crossing can accompany the folded arms position or be displayed on its own. It isn't necessarily a negative position. You have to look for the clusters. Women were often told from an early age that it was the correct way to sit. If accompanied by folded arms, however, it can be a negative/defensive signal. If you're trying to make a point to somebody or sell a product, for example, it's difficult to look enthusiastic with your arms folded and/or legs crossed. And it's not very convincing for the other person. **An open position is necessary**.

- When someone remains slouched in a chair when you walk in, rather than getting up to greet you, the impression given is not favourable. Some interviewers are guilty of doing this. You may have come across this at work when going to see your boss. It doesn't make you feel good. It can be used to make you feel inferior or that you're a time-waster.

- Do you sometimes sit with both hands behind your head? You may do it unconsciously, because you happen to be feeling good and everything's going your way. But, as was stressed earlier on in the chapter, *it's the effect that your body language has on other people that you need to be aware of.* This gesture is often used by people who are feeling superior or confident (for example, a manager who is feeling great because he's telling the person whom he's been dying to get rid of that his employment is terminated), but it can be extremely offensive or irritating to the onlooker. It can be interpreted as aggressive and conveys to the other person that you don't see them as a threat.

  Open hand and body gestures are generally used to convey a positive, friendly attitude to the speaker. If you're trying to influence somebody to agree to a course of action or persuade them of something, **use open gestures: time and time again, they have been shown to be the most effective**.

- Another sitting gesture is possibly one that you've used in trying to get away from a relative or well-meaning friend. You know the one I mean: where you either grip the chair as if to go, or lean forward with your hands on your knees. But you never quite make it because either another anecdote comes out or another home-made fruit scone is offered.

In business, this is a valuable pointer to your next move. The other person is satisfied and is waiting for you to move on to the next step or wants to end the session (they may have another meeting to attend or other things to do). If there is a negative reason, you will have picked this up by observing other cluster leaks. It would pay you to make the first move and initiate the ending of the meeting with whatever follow-up is necessary. It can cause frustration if a person signals to you to end the encounter and you don't pick it up or take heed. They then have to start the ritual all over again. This can engender negative feelings.

- Sitting perched on the edge of your chair creates a nervous impression. It can indicate to the other person that you don't really want to be there. It could be because you are nervous yourself, or that you haven't really got the time or perhaps the inclination. Either way, it doesn't create a favourable impression.

Other gestures

There are a whole host of other body signals that can be misinterpreted (or interpreted correctly). You'll see people who, while apparently paying attention to you, are tapping their feet, peering over their glasses, touching their nose, rubbing their eyes or ears, touching their mouth, clenching their hands, drumming their fingertips, blinking a lot, playing with their hair, playing with jewellery or a watch, rocking in their chair, playing with pens or looking at their fingernails excessively. These are just a few mannerisms that could be giving out negative vibes. Watch out for them, and check your own body language.

So, an important point to remember is this:

> **It is usually our extremities that give us away (as we have the least control over our hands and feet).**

Spatial relationships

Posture can be an indicator of the intensity of a person's emotions when part of a cluster. If someone changes the subject to a confidential topic, they may alter their body position to bring the other person closer. People tend to lean forward, towards each other, when there is a degree of respect or liking.

An important aspect of body-language analysis is the concept of spatial relationships; in other words, your **personal-space** preferences, which dictate the *distance* from people at which you are comfortable. The closer the proximity, the more intimate that relationship will tend to be. Psychologists have identified four distinct zones:

- *Intimate*: up to about 18 inches from the body. It will include close friends, spouse and family.

- *Personal*: roughly split into two subzones of 18–30 inches, which can include spouse, close friends and work colleagues you may know well, and 30–48 inches, which is quite close proximity, found when conversing with people at a party, for example. It's interesting to watch how, at a social or work gathering, the arrival of an 'infiltrator' may cause people to step back and adjust their personal 'bubble'. Another person may swivel round to talk to someone else, for example. If the person passes the 'initiation' and stays in the group, then people start to move closer again and the dynamics return to their previous state.

- *Social*: from 4–12 feet, the distance between people who do not know each other that well. It could apply to a seminar situation or a distance from someone higher in the hierarchy at work.

- *Public*: upwards of 12 feet. This is a comfortable distance for being with strangers. If you're speaking at a meeting, this is the zone you would feel comfortable with, as far as distance from your audience is concerned. If it's a small group you are addressing then the distance may be shorter.

It appears that most of us are quite happy to engage in conversations within the personal zone. In business or other formal circumstances, the social zone seems to be used. **We all have our own personal space 'bubble' that surrounds us and follows us around**. It is as well to remember this when interacting with new acquaintances.

Just a word about public transport (buses, trains, underground) before I leave your personal space. All rules seem to go out of the window when it comes to public transport – as well as theatres, lifts and other crowd situations. 'Whatever happened to my intimate and personal space bubble?' I can almost hear you cry.

Well, it doesn't exist and so we go through a whole ritual of body language **defensive** displays to **compensate** for the invasion in these crowded public spaces. In the lift, for example, we'll remain silent, avoid eye contact, immerse ourselves in reading material or watch in awe as the floor numbers are illuminated from floor to floor! It's the same on public transport. *We don't acknowledge the existence of these people*, who, if we did, we would consider to have trespassed on to our two most private zones.

Talking of 'private zones', I'd just like to share with you a conversation I had with my psychology professor many years ago when I was trying to define the behavioural aspects of psychology in relation to the cognitive (mind). I asked him what he considered to be the *definition* of a psychologist. He paused, in a way that only serious academics can do, and then said to me:

> **'A psychologist is someone who goes to a striptease show and spends most of the time watching the audience.'**

So make sure you spend most of your time watching your audience and their body language – and being aware of your own.

An understanding of the communication of bodily movements used when people interact with each other – the science of 'kinesics' – is an important one. Hopefully, as well as observing *other people's* non-verbal behaviour, you'll have realized that you should

always be saying to yourself: 'What is the impression I am sending with *my* body language?' And, more importantly, 'Is this what I want?' **Make sure your body is talking the right language**.

Coffee break . . .

The impressions you m_____ and those you r_____ are influenced heavily by non-verbal behaviours.

Around ____ per cent of our impact during any encounter comes from verbal and non-verbal aspects of speech; the other _____ per cent is non-verbal 'body language'.

This verbal aspect is termed p_____.

We tend to trust and be influenced much more by people whose facial expressions are c_____ with (i.e. match) the words that come out of their mouth.

Time and time again, good e_____ c_____ comes out as a very important non-verbal means of promoting good interpersonal communication.

It doesn't matter what a particular g_____ of your own means to you; it's how the other person perceives it that's important.

If you're trying to influence somebody to agree to a course of action, o___ hand and body gestures have been shown to be the most effective.

There are a whole host of body signals that can be misinterpreted – so always look for 'c_____' of gestures rather than one in isolation.

Remember – the mind and body are one: you cannot not c_____.

Chapter

5

'Life is *all* memory except for the one present moment that goes by you so quick you hardly catch it going.'

Tennessee Williams

Memory magic

The impact of good recall and simple tips to improve your memory

- 'Ah yes, I remember it well ...'
- Coding
- Remembering names
- Interest is flattering
- Making associations
- Introductions
- Rule 1: make sure that you hear the name
- Rule 2: if you hear a name, make sure you put it to the right face
- The importance of names
- Business cards can be trumps
- Empty promises? 'You *cannot* be serious!'
- Remembering figures
- Remembering telephone numbers
- The importance of memory in controlling attention

Aside from expressing a desire to become more persuasive, as far as the next 'wish-list' attribute that most people would like, a good memory is always near the top of the list. Life is *all* memory. Of course, having a good memory with powerful recall is an effective tool for being persuasive in your dealings with people. We don't have to think hard to imagine how a better memory would enhance our lives on a day-to-day level in the workplace and with family and friends. How do you feel when you can't remember things?

A poor memory threatens everything in life: personal relationships, business contacts, income, health – the list is endless.

'My wife went ballistic with me . . . I didn't hear her tell me that last week . . .'

'The client will probably drop us now – how was I supposed to know . . .?'

'I was really embarrassed . . . it completely slipped my mind that she paid the last time we ate there . . .'

'I was already tense at the interview, so I just could not remember what . . .'

'I kept calling him Ken during the meeting because I'm sure that's how they introduced him. I don't remember his name as Matthew, that's for sure . . .'

'Yes, at the annual Christmas party I knew the faces of those people in accounts, I just didn't have a clue of their names . . . I suppose as MD I should have checked . . . you don't think they were offended – I mean . . . err . . .'

Any of these sound remotely familiar? Ouch!

'Ah yes, I remember it well . . .'

Well, we do think we remember things well – as the song goes . . .

'We met at nine'
'We met at eight'
'I was on time'
'No, you were late'
'Ah yes, I remember it well . . .'

'That carriage ride'
'You walked me home'
'You lost a glove'
'I lost a comb'
'Ah yes, I remember it well . . .'

'That brilliant sky'
'We had some rain'
'Those Russian songs'
'From sunny Spain'
'Ah yes, I remember it well . . .' ♫

But the sad truth is that most people pay little attention to improving their memory skills and consequently put up with faulty recall.

Most of what we say is founded on something that has happened, something that we did or that somebody else did. So, if your recall of your own valuable experiences or others' words of wisdom is that bit better than the average person's, then you're bound to come out on top. When people are questioned about the attributes they would like that they don't believe they possess, a good memory is always near the top of the list.

The problem is that a lot of people have very *average* memories and many others have very *bad* ones. If you can break from this mould, you're in a very powerful position. In business and personal life, the confidence that comes from a good power of recall is valuable beyond measure. And we all have it within us to improve our memories and therefore our lives.

Let's take a quick look at the way in which cognitive psychologists like to compare the human mind to a computer, and memory to an information-processing system. In today's IT world, the analogy affords a useful way to see how 'breakdown' can occur in the system. The PC receives input from the keyboard: it converts the symbols to a numeric code; the information is saved on the disk; information is retrieved from your disk either by displaying it on the computer screen or printing it out. If there's a breakdown in the system, or there's not enough disk space, or you delete the file, you'll find that the information has been 'forgotten', as you're unable to access it.

Following on from this, researchers in the field of memory have attempted to look at the way in which any information that we receive is processed mentally, in the information-processing system. In this context, a stimulus that registers in our sensory system will be remembered only if it (a) draws **attention**, which brings it into consciousness, (b) becomes **encoded** in the brain and **stored**, and (c) is **retrieved** for use at some later stage.

Furthermore, to optimize our memory capability we need to engage both sides of the brain; in other words, the logical (left) and the creative (right) side. As you will see later, this involves the use of **association** and **mnemonics**.

Three types of memory thus become identified: sensory, short-term and long-term.

Sensory memory

This refers to things that are stored for a very brief period of time, ranging from a fraction of a second to perhaps three seconds. This form of memory is difficult to distinguish from the act of perception. For example, it would contain an image of something just glimpsed or a fleeting sound that was just heard. The sensations that do not draw attention simply disappear, as no analysis is performed on the information; those sensations that are 'noticed' are transferred to the next form of memory, short-term memory.

Short-term memory

This is a very interesting side of memory cognition. The key to it is **attention**. Short-term memory has a limited storage facility in terms of the number of items it can store and in duration; in other words, it is limited in the amount of information it can store and how long it can store it for.

Research into how many items a person can store with correct recall has shown a figure of seven (plus or minus two), whether they be numbers, names, letters or words. Short-term memory has its limits, and rightly so. Going back to the computer and information-processing model, it is like removing old and unwanted files from your disk. Can you imagine the situation if you couldn't clear unwanted items from your short-term memory? Your mind would contain trivia such as your lottery numbers of three weeks ago, unwanted telephone numbers, every sensation that you'd ever experienced.

Recall usually relies on **repetition** and **rehearsal**, otherwise the information can disappear just as quickly as it entered your consciousness. For example, you may hear a telephone number on the radio, dash to the phone (there's no pen handy, of course), and as you get to the fifth digit you have to hang up because the rest of the number has gone from your head. Or you're at a party and, while you're chatting to somebody you met 20 minutes ago, your partner comes over; as you introduce him to your new acquaintance you can't remember her name.

The repetition method (or 'maintenance rehearsal', as memory researchers have termed it) of repeating the information silently (or aloud if circumstances allow it) would have helped in both these instances. Rehearsal is used to maintain the information in the short-term memory indefinitely.

Long-term memory

You can rehearse information in your short-term memory until it eventually becomes stored in your long-term memory. This contains information that is thought about in a more meaningful and deeper way and is associated with other knowledge that is already stored in the long-term memory ('**elaborative rehearsal**'). Unlike short-term memory, long-term memory has no known limits. Information stored here does not become lost if it isn't retrieved or rehearsed. It can be called up as needed.

An important aspect of elaborative rehearsal in long-term memory is the linking of new information to the self. The self, in other words, can be used as a memory aid. **You're relating**

information to what you *already* know – forming associations. You elaborate on new information by recollecting information that you already have stored in your long-term memory.

If we process any new information as relevant to our own experiences, we consider the information in a deeper fashion and our recall is improved vastly. If you met someone at a party who had the same birthday as you – month, date and year – wouldn't you be more likely to remember them and their name than someone whom you perhaps found equally interesting? If a prospective client went to the same university as you, there's a good chance you might remember that, even if you didn't see them again for a few years and you bumped into them later. True, you might have remembered the face – with long-term memory certain types of data, such as people's faces, are encoded without any conscious effort – but you may also know their name, where you met them and what university they graduated from. (If the other person's memory is poor or average, they'll be astounded that you remembered which university they attended – but how you did it is your secret!)

Coding

Information is stored in two fashions or 'codes'. These have important implications in terms of improving our memories. First, there is **semantic** coding. Any verbal communication is processed in terms of the *meaning* of the communication as a whole, not the specific words that made up the message. For example:

John (to his colleague, Janice): 'So, I had to tell Mrs Hughes that if we don't get the post room to speed up delivery to individual departments, she'll have to hire somebody to come in at 7 a.m. to do a preliminary sort, to make things quicker for the boys when they get in at 8 a.m.'

Janice (recounting John's conversation later on): 'John's going to get somebody in at seven if things don't improve. He's cleared it with his boss.'

Sally: 'Look, Dad. If I don't get a mobile phone, then if the train's late or breaks down, I'm going to find it difficult letting you know when to pick me up from the station. Those telephone boxes never work . . . Susan's mum gave her and Alice one as presents last month.'

Dad (talking to his wife that evening): 'Yes, she says it's handy if the trains are delayed, or whatever, for letting us know. Her friend Susan and her sister got them as presents for Christmas or something. I don't think we can get out of it.'

So, it's the *semantic* construction that is stored, with a fair dose of reading between the lines so that we recall not just what we thought we heard but also what was implied during part of the message. In the second example above, the father said his daughter's friend had got one for Christmas; in fact, she just mentioned 'presents'.

Most verbal information is stored in our long-term memory in a semantic way. Visual inputs and many other items of information are more likely to be stored as visual images. Using **imagery** to remember things, as research constantly shows, is highly effective. Forming an image of words and relating them in an interactive way with something else that needs to be remembered is a common technique that people use.

The key is to make it *memorable*. Say you had to remember to (a) post a letter and (b) pick up your dry-cleaning on the way to (c) taking your car in to the garage for a service and (d) asking the mechanic for the umbrella you left there when you dashed in a few days earlier – you might form a mental image covering all four intended actions, an interactive one that relates all four activities. And, because it's in your imagination, it can be as bizarre as you like.

Your first image might be a post box (a); then an image of you wearing a dry-cleaned suit with the plastic covers still on it (b); then a scene with your car in the garage forecourt (c); with your umbrella hooked over the steering-wheel like one of those security devices (d). All of these images could be connected in your mind by a picture of you sitting in the driving seat of your car wearing a suit with the dry-cleaning cover on it; in front of you, your steering-wheel is 'locked' with your umbrella, and there is a post box perched on the roof of your car. Just *one* image now. Rehearse it in your mind a few times (don't tell anybody about it!); after it has enabled you to carry out the functions, jettison it from your memory. Mission accomplished.

On a practical, everyday level, it is probably now clear that most problems relating to a person's poor or average recall relate to what happens when they're *encoding* information. Encoding means actually getting this material into memory. Psychologists prove continually that the process of retrieval is enhanced considerably by frequent rehearsal.

Some information that was unrehearsed gets encoded and stored into the memory with very little attention or effort. This is known as **automatic processing**. But, as we have seen, most material cannot be encoded successfully unless **attention** is paid to it.

How we encode the information directly affects our chances of *remembering* it. Giving the information some personal meaning reduces the likelihood that we will forget it.

Remembering names

You've said it to yourself a thousand times: '*I remember the face, but I can't remember the name.*' Remembering names appears to be the biggest problem for most people, especially in the working world. And yet the name is the most important piece of information that we need to know about an individual. If you forget somebody's name, you're aiming a knockdown shot at the ego – and it's a bull's-eye. Although it might not be made obvious, you've lost a few points immediately. Your faux pas may register only in the other person's subconscious, but it is still significant.

In most cases, it's not that you actually *forget* a name. You probably never picked it up in the first place because you failed to hear it properly and did nothing to rectify this. This could be because:

- it is an interest problem – you just weren't interested enough to fully catch the person's name and 'store' it;
- you were distracted at the time of the introduction because your mind was elsewhere.

Whatever the reason, it's not good enough. Remembering names is such a potent social skill or persuasion tool that, if you do nothing else, you must make the effort to improve in this area. When you use somebody's name, you find that you receive more attention; it's human nature. Whatever '**two-timing**' in terms of straying thoughts may be going on in our heads, at the mention of our name our ears prick up.

You'll notice this when you're out shopping, or at your bank or building society, or eating in a restaurant. The widespread use of credit cards, cheques and loyalty cards has led to organizations referring to people by name to add a personal touch. Hotels and airline check-in desks have been doing this for years, of course:

'I hope you enjoy your meal, Miss . . .'

'Wish you a pleasant flight, Mr . . .'

'Any problems with the toaster, Miss . . . , please bring it back to us.'

'I hope the room's OK for you, Miss . . . Just call down to reception if you'd like to change.'

'How would you like your money, Mr . . .?'

They've realized the success of such a basic appeal to vanity. It's a caressing of the ego that works wonders. It's just a simple gesture – but it can have a great effect, because people like to be recognized as individuals. They go back to places where people know them.

Canny people in any business make a point of committing names to memory. There is no better way of creating the beginnings of a **rapport** with someone than being interested enough to remember their name. Have you noticed in your love life how it works wonders? Or when you're returning something faulty to a store and you've remembered the name of the person that served you? (OK – you found it on the bill.) Or when you're in a business meeting with more than one person and you remember the names of the 'least important' members of the meeting? (Hey, they can influence too, you know.) Arguments, points of view and business generally have been won or lost because a person's name was remembered or forgotten.

You can improve yourself mentally, just as you can improve your physique from working out in the gym. Everyone has the ability. Become your own personal trainer. Conditioning the mind through mental jogging can help develop a more effective memory for names.

Interest is flattering

If you remember something about a person, they feel flattered: you're appealing to their ego.

'You were going to see *Les Miserables* the last time I saw you. How was it?'

'When we spoke in March, you'd just exchanged contracts on your house. Have you moved in yet?'

'You were having problems with the contractors over your new offices the last time we met. Sorted out now?'

To make way for valuable information to be stored in our memory, as we observed earlier on in this chapter, it's necessary to '**de-clutter**' it. You have to relegate useless information to your own personal recycle bin. There are people who can give you the Wimbledon Singles Champions since 1972 but can't remember their car number plate. They can recite the last ten minutes of *Gone With the Wind* but wouldn't have a hope of remembering their bank PIN. A readjustment is needed.

Remember, the first essential is a conscious effort to be *interested*. One person's lack of knowledge about another results from no effort being made to take an interest. Even in a lot of friendships, empathy and understanding can sadly be a one-way affair. Some people are so superficial in their dealings with others that the conversation often goes something like this:

'How's things, Mark?'

'Well, business isn't that good at the moment. And I had a burglary last week . . .'

'Good, good . . . I wanted to ask if you might . . .'

How can you possibly *remember* things if you don't programme your mind to register what the other person is saying? It's selfishness, really. If you want something from another person – friendship, a job, a sale, help, money, sympathy, assistance – you've got to be interested enough to remember things connected with them. It allows you to establish a productive two-way relationship.

The simplest way to improve memory is by **association**. You may come across people with whom you have something in common; this ought to help you to remember facts about them. It could be many things: age, birthplace, love of a sport, car, a holiday, a name, a whole host of possible things. This common factor can easily trigger a memory association. And since the other person's memory isn't that good, they will have *forgotten* they ever told you about their new car, holiday, recent accident, etc. As a result, when you say, 'How's your Ferrari running?' or 'Played any tennis lately?' or 'How was Sardinia?' or 'Is your husband better?' they can't help but be surprised – and impressed; 'How did you know . . . ?'

Making associations

If you were shown 150 photographs of celebrities from the entertainment world and public life, the chances are that you might be able to name upwards of 130. And yet you probably have not met even *one* of these people.

You recognized their faces and you remembered their names. The reason is that you're interested in retaining the name and used (unconsciously) whatever associations you needed to remember it. If you were shown a photograph of the actress Elizabeth Taylor in the role of Cleopatra, it's probably Cleopatra that makes you remember her name (or possibly the other way round).

We are all more proficient in *recognizing* than *recalling*, **which explains why quite often we'll remember a face but not the name**. The secret of remembering names lies with the individual. It's back to your own imagination again. Certain names you will remember without difficulty:

- Those people who are important in your daily life. You'll naturally remember the names of your relatives, friends, work colleagues, business clients, your doctor, your bank manager, etc.

- Those people who have had a great influence on your life. For example, your old headteacher, the person who interviewed you for your first job, the person who handed you the lottery cheque for £1.4 million, and the driving examiner who enabled you to tear up your L-plates when you passed your driving test.

But what about the people we come across whose names we would *like* to remember – socially or perhaps during a business meeting? The problem's the same, although it's more crucial in a formal business setting.

Many names, at least surnames, can be significant to us. We can equate them with something and paint word pictures. Names such as Harper, Walker and Shepherd – they're easy. With names like Longman, Royle and Silver, an association could easily be formed.

Now, we must get one thing straight: your imagination belongs to *you*. Some people feel almost guilty at devising silly associations in their heads. I can understand the concern. What goes on in your mind is your affair. If you devise daft methods of remembering names, and it helps you in your life, then go ahead.

Let's take the examples above. For Harper, you could picture a person playing a harp. Walker: perhaps visualize a person with a rucksack. Shepherd: a person with a sheep in their arms. Longman: picture the person as a circus l-o-n-g man. Royle: imagine the person with a crown on their head. Silver: imagine the person with a black patch over one eye. The possibilities are endless, and begin and end with you.

If these visual pictures don't prompt your memory, nothing will. Picture individuals in this way and make a point of registering the pictures in your mind. Then, when you look at these people, it will be to the accompaniment of your finely tuned imagination. If we want something to be memorable, it's a great help if it's *imaginative*. (Neuropsychologists have shown that memory and imagination use both sides of the brain.)

While they're frantically trying to remember a person's name, you'll be reeling off theirs; it will trip off the tongue. They won't know how you do it (which may be just as well!).

But you know how. *It's magic.* The magic of memory.

Introductions

Often, as we discussed earlier, it's not a case of forgetting a name. It's rather that it simply *didn't register* in the first place. This is nothing more than laziness or disinterest. Or nerves. Nerves? Why nerves?

It seems that when we meet people for the first time, the momentary shock to the system diverts us from our normal listening process. We're so aware of what we're going to say, what we look like and the impression we are giving that we miss the name when it's announced. So, it's not that we've *forgotten* the name a few seconds later; **it's more likely that we just didn't hear it**. But the other person doesn't always know that. And quite often they won't give you the benefit of the doubt. Especially if they've heard and remembered your name.

If you don't catch somebody's name at the outset (or if it simply isn't given), then the few seconds of handshake (if that's the formal type of situation you're in) afford ample opportunity to ask the other person to **repeat** it. There is a general reluctance, almost embarrassment, about doing this for fear of seeming rude or daft. On the contrary, it demonstrates politeness. Our names are the most personal things we possess – they're unique to us. A name forms a big part in the psychology of the self. Consequently, people are often more responsive to those who use them.

Two people are introduced to each other by a third party. They shake hands:

'Hello. I'm Sue Madsen.'

'Pleased to meet you. John Watkins.'

It sounds straightforward, but one or the other or both of these people are capable of missing the name because of the concern or worry of *what to say next*. As they are being introduced, their minds are simultaneously working on the next sentence. The name can be blotted out. It's not a memory problem in this case; it's a *hearing* problem.

Think back to a party you've been to. On arrival, a bottle of Cabernet Sauvignon in hand, you are confronted with a roomful of faces. You're introduced to a string of people. One by one, names are reeled off: 'Richard – this is Eileen, Simon, Sheila, Paul, Lisa, Andrew, Rachael . . .'

At the same time, you are trying to take in many other aspects of the scene – the decor, the people in the background, the music, how much wine there is left and anything else that catches your eye.

These **distractions**, combined with your own self-consciousness at meeting all these new people, mean that you probably catch only one or two names, if that. And even then you don't always attach the right *name* to the right *face*. It's not so bad for the people you're being introduced to. *They have only one name to remember at the time – yours*. Also, they have already established their territory, so they're more relaxed. *It's much easier to remember things when you're relaxed.*

You probably end up gravitating initially towards the two people whose names you happened to pick up. Just your luck – *the two biggest bores* – those awful smartass types who have taken out their own appendix or done their own conveyancing when selling their house.

Rule 1: make sure that you hear the name

Imagine that you arrive at the office of a client, Mr Good, for a meeting with him and three other members of his division, including his boss, the managing director, Mr King.

As you enter the boardroom, your contact Mr Good introduces you to his three colleagues: 'Nice to see you again. I'd like to introduce you to Simon King our managing director, Jason Mollet from publicity and Annette Barnes from information technology.'

You fail to hear Mr King's name at all. As you shift your briefcase uneasily from your right to your left hand, in readiness to shake his hand, you mutter: 'Er . . . How d'you do?' You manage to catch the names Mollet and Barnes: 'How do you do, Mr Mollet, Miss Barnes?'

You're shown to a seat and the discussion starts. Mr Good had mentioned on a previous occasion that his boss, Mr King, was the one with the ultimate authority to give a go-ahead; the decision-maker. Nothing could be agreed, he'd said, unless the managing director went along with it. But his boss was apparently a reasonable man – a 'people person' – who liked to know he was dealing with somebody with integrity and empathy, somebody he could trust. Hence, the group meeting in which he wanted to be present.

Since you can't remember Mr King's name, you find yourself addressing Mr Mollet, *whose name you did catch*, and also your original contact, Mr Good. (Your short-term memory registered the name Mollet because you remember a girl Molly that you once knew; that, plus rehearsal and good mental imagery, meant that remembering his name was no problem throughout the meeting.) Mr Good happens to be the least influential member of the group as far as this project is concerned. *Yet you end up directing most of your points and questions to him*. Why? Because you know his name and find yourself automatically veering towards him.

Mr King and Miss Barnes are not given as much attention. Yet *they* are the two people with the power to agree to the proposal. It is with them that you should have been trying hard to establish a level of empathy and rapport.

This scenario occurs every day in business meetings and socially. It does not promote effective communication. But it's so easy to avoid. And what positive results are achieved by doing so!

It's so simple. At the start, the obvious statement 'I'm sorry, I didn't catch your name' would have been the solution. But most people don't do it. Why? People seem to assume that the attitude of the other person is: 'Either you get my name the first time or forget it.' As though it's an unforgivable faux pas. As though the person who has dared to ask for the name to be repeated should be written off as slow, stupid or unprofessional, or all three.

Don't ever feel embarrassed about admitting that you didn't hear a name. There's a two-fold advantage to this:

- You are actually sure of the name.
- As a psychological plus, you make the person you are meeting *feel more important*. You've shown that you consider knowing their name worthwhile.

Rule 2: if you hear a name, make sure you put it to the right face

If you have ever got people's names crossed during a meeting or in a social situation, it's probably something you won't want to repeat. The embarrassment can be so great that if you are ever in any doubt then it is often better to use no name at all. Otherwise this will definitely reduce your effectiveness as a communicator whose aim is to create rapport with a particular set of individuals. Certainly, calling the person by the *wrong* name is infinitely worse than not remembering the name at all.

The importance of names

If you want to test how much importance you subconsciously attach to names in a work situation, catch yourself when you're at a conference, exhibition, seminar or whatever. Visitors and delegates are probably wearing the obligatory plastic name badges. You spot a familiar face but can't remember the name. That may deter you in the first instance from actually going up for a chat. If you do, you probably end up not concentrating on the conversation because intermittently (and subtly – or so you think) *you're trying to sneak a look at the name on the badge*.

She's remembered *your* name and *your* company. That's put even more stress on you. You feel terribly embarrassed. You've been so intent on trying to read her name badge – but the light's been shining on the plastic and you couldn't see – that you've missed most of what she's said. She asks you a question related to the discussion. You're at a loss because you haven't been listening. This looks like lack of interest. She thinks you're a waste of time and moves off, politely, at the earliest opportunity.

You still didn't get her name. And now she's got the wrong impression about you, on top of everything else.

Sometimes it pays to ask somebody else, discreetly, the name of the person concerned: 'My memory's going. Who's that over there?' If you don't know the person that well, and it's quite acceptable that it has slipped your mind (i.e. it wouldn't cause offence), then 'Sorry, your name's escaped me' – or the equivalent – is permissible. Sometimes, through good fortune, the person in question, if in a group, will automatically shake hands with a new arrival and identify themselves. That solves your problem.

Business cards can be trumps

As we've seen, in the sometimes extremely formal set-tings of work encounters, getting names right can be crucial. Fortunately, we're sometimes helped with the common currency of the world of work: the business card. These are almost universal ('Could I have your card?' or 'Here's my card'), yet there are some people who take great delight in not having them, precisely because they are in such common use. But there's no question that a card can be useful, for a number of reasons:

- It establishes the image of you or your company.

- It supplies your name and status at the outset.

- It can provide an interesting opener when you meet someone, and it establishes initial ice-breaking conversation.

- From the memory aspect, it solves your immediate short-term memory challenge, as you have the card in front of you in case you forget the person's name in the course of your conversation.

People vary in their preferences about when to hand over a business card. Offering your own card at the beginning of a meeting generally helps the other person to remember your name and to evaluate your status. They will usually reciprocate, allowing you to confirm or evaluate their position too. But some people hand over their cards at the end of a meeting.

If you think you'll have trouble remembering the person's name, or are unsure of it, then be sure to exchange cards at the start, when you arrive. Then keep theirs in view so that you can refer to it. They are probably doing the same with yours. It's on the desk in front of them, or on the sofa beside them if the seating is informal. They don't want to get your name wrong either.

Empty promises? 'You *cannot* be serious!'

A particularly disturbing habit that people exhibit in their everyday lives causes more upsets and misunderstandings than anything else – family feuds, divorces, friends falling out with each other and fractured business relationships are typical casualties. What causes them? The making of empty promises and statements.

In many cases, the person who is *promised* something that does not materialize *forgets* anyway, so no harm is done. Relationships continue and business keeps functioning. But in many instances, what turned out to be empty words are *forgotten* by the speaker but *remembered* by the listener. This does not make for harmonious relationships.

Consider this situation in a workplace setting involving a potential client:

'Well, I'll see you next month after the two-week event is over.'

'What are you doing exactly?'

'Wimbledon. We're putting together some corporate events there over the two weeks. John McEnroe will be involved in a couple of things with us.'

'Oh. You *cannot* be serious! Ha! We've never managed to get tickets. Lucky you. My wife loves tennis – my daughter too.'

'I'll get a programme for your wife – I'll get McEnroe to sign it. How old's your daughter?'

'Samantha? She's eleven.'

'I'll get you a Wimbledon T-shirt. Signed programme for your wife and a T-shirt for your daughter.'

'Hey, I don't want to put you through any trouble or . . .'

'No – no. It'll be my pleasure – and my treat.'

'Well – they'll be really chuffed. That's extremely kind of you.'

'That's OK. I'll see you sometime in July then, and I'll have all the figures and costs documented and we can take things a stage further.'

'Great. Hope you have a good time at the tennis – don't forget your umbrella in reception.'

'No – and I won't forget it for Wimbledon either! Bye.'

Typically, our man has forgotten this conversation by the time he gets back to the visitors' car park, where he receives a couple of mobile-phone messages relating to various problems back at the office. The potential client he has just been to see has a good memory. He even tells his wife that evening that a 'great guy' he was dealing with would be getting them a signed Wimbledon programme and later tells his daughter she'll be getting a T-shirt. They're both really pleased.

Three weeks later, this 'nice guy' returns from his travels and arranges a follow-up meeting. The conversation goes as follows:

'Well, how was Wimbledon? Great second week wasn't it?'

Our man is flattered. He feels important. 'What a great guy', he thinks. (Reader: didn't we hear that somewhere else before?) 'He remembers I was going off to Wimbledon. I can't remember telling him about the tennis.'

'Have you ever been there?'

'Er . . . no. D'you remember me saying the last time you were here that we've always been unlucky with tickets?'

'Oh, err . . . err . . . That's right. Of course. You've . . . err . . . got a brother who likes tennis.' (It's obvious from his facial expressions

and the rest of his body language that he doesn't remember, or that the recollection is very very vague.)

The disillusioned potential client is now doubting our man's integrity, has decided he's very superficial and is disappointed at his lack of sincerity. During the rest of the meeting there is no mention of the 'gifts' that had been promised so effusively.

The client makes his final evaluation of his visitor as he escorts him to the lift.

'Can we go ahead and make preparations based on the figures I've given you?'

'You *cannot* be serious!' (Lift door closes.)

Apart from feeling angry at the man's lack of self-awareness, he also decides that the man is insincere. His inner feeling is: 'If you can forget this, then if I do business with you you'll forget to give me good customer service after I sign the contract – oh, and you probably also forgot to tell me the drawbacks of your service!' The moral is: **woe betide you and your broken promises if the other person has a good memory. You'll come unstuck**.

Come on: get inside the other person's mind. Forgetting a throw-away line – which was quite incidental to the conversation – may seem a trivial thing to you. But it may be *significant* to the other person involved.

What message does it send out about your character and integrity? It's important to remember: different people have very different levels of sensitivity.

Casual remarks or promises that may seem unimportant to you may strike a chord with the other person. You're then expected to come up with the goods. If you fail to do so, your true worth as a person is in doubt – and it becomes hard to alter that judgement. In situations like the example given, the client would use such behaviour as a barometer of the other person's trustworthiness.

A poor memory can destroy relationships. But it's an *interest* problem, so it can be cured. **Simply take more interest in whatever is important to the other person**. You must make the effort to pick up people's reactions to what you are saying or doing, in any kind of relationship.

More often than not, the other party will not convey their real feelings about your sins of omission (as in the above example). Your forgetfulness or thoughtlessness is quite likely to result in a rift. You can lose a friend or you can lose business. *And you may not even know why*.

Take some everyday situations:

● A friend lends you £10 to save you queuing at the bank. You forget to pay her back.

- Another friend buys your theatre ticket for *Phantom of the Opera*, as you've left your credit card in the car. You forget to pay her back.

- Your secretary works late to get important reports typed up for you. You promise to buy her a bottle of 'bubbly' for her kindness. You forget.

- You tell a client that you'll call on Friday with the name of a good physiotherapist for his backache. You forget.

Do these situations jog any personal memories? Have you been there? You may have been the perpetrator *or* on the receiving end. Nobody wants the embarrassment of reminding you that you have not paid your debts or fulfilled your promises. You should make a point of remembering in the first place what you commit yourself to. Otherwise you may find eventually that people have no time for you. They give you the cold shoulder. And you can't think why.

You can't even raid your memory bank to work out the reason – because it's permanently on overdraft. You never put anything in!

Remembering figures

In our normal lives we benefit greatly from being able to remember figures, but in a business context it assumes even greater importance – dates, prices, technical details. This really should be no problem even for the person with a so-called bad memory. It's just a question of making a conscious effort, e.g. by linking the figures with other figures that already mean something to you. The process is shown in Figure 5.1.

Remembering telephone numbers

Association makes it much easier to recall telephone numbers too. It just requires a little deep thinking. There are certain phone numbers that are etched in our memories – those of relatives, friends, certain business contacts, doctor's surgery, bank, pizza delivery service. But how often are you caught out because you can't remember a number? And so you don't make the call. You'll make it 'later'. Result: end of a relationship, lost business, friction – and more. All because you haven't made a conscious effort to remember a number.

So, again, first be interested in memorizing the number. Then look for a way of remembering it **by relating it to something you already know**. Then, when you're trying to recall, your mind will link the two things together.

For example, consider the number: 021 394568. Your imagination provides you with a way of remembering 021 – perhaps how

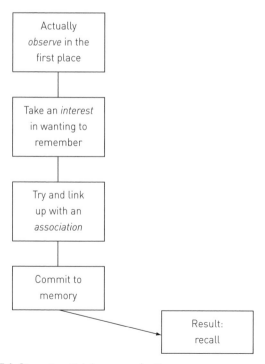

Figure 5.1 Steps to attaining a productive memory

old you were when you graduated – and 3945 happens to be the years when the Second World War started and ended; 68 may be an old flat number of yours as a student. So, you've associated a telephone number that you would like to recall at will with facts that you already know. You have programmed your mind. (Test: see if you can remember this number in 59 minutes' time.)

Let's take another example: the phone number of a client, Tom Beechwood, is 65549. For the person's name, you could imagine a wooden table made of beech wood. Then think of retirement age being 65; 54 might be the year of your birth, while 9 may be your lucky number. Connect these in your mind and see how easy it is. But remember, *be interested enough to want to remember it*. (Test: see if you can remember this in 60 minutes' time.)

(Note: when you've amazed yourself at how competent you've suddenly become at memorizing these example numbers, jettison them from your psyche and **substitute** them with two telephone numbers that you've never been able – or bothered – to commit to memory.)

The importance of memory in controlling attention

In a business situation, you may frequently need to remember prices, discounts and other figures relating to various products and services. Of course, there is usually a price list of some sort that you may be able to refer to, which means that most businesspeople do not take the time or trouble to commit such figures to memory.

But what about when you need to think on your feet? Being able to remember prices/rates without recourse to written material can often mean the difference between a deal and no deal.

How? Well, it's all tied up with the **attention curve**, which you'll remember from Chapter 3. (Now there's a memory test for you!) Remember the importance of timing in a meeting: how an interruption can disturb that emotional high, that fleeting moment that is make or break. Everything that you've said or done before has been leading up to this psychological 'hot spot' of the proceedings. Successful deals are struck at this point. You're asked a question about price, discounts or specifications, and your eye contact is suspended as you look away and ponder over written material. The spell is broken, just as when the television commercial appears as the car is heading towards the edge of the cliff.

If you were able to memorize prices, for example, you wouldn't have to look away. When the other person asks, 'What would be the air-time rate for three consecutive slots on a weekday and two on a Saturday evening, prime-time?' instead of **breaking the dialogue** to rummage through price lists and rate cards, you can answer immediately. You're giving the other person minimal opportunity to lose concentration and, more importantly, for their emotional state to change.

Most people do not realize how potent the use of memory is at this sensitive stage.

Don't break the dialogue. Come out with your facts and figures naturally and maintain that eye contact. Keep the attention span constant. It's a precious commodity.

The potential attention curves for a situation with and without a break are illustrated in Figure 5.2. These show how efficient use of memory can change the level of the proceedings.

Memory can be influenced by a number of factors, such as age, laziness, disinterest, distraction, stress, fatigue, alcohol and lack of confidence. The following is an interesting observation in Jane Austen's writing:

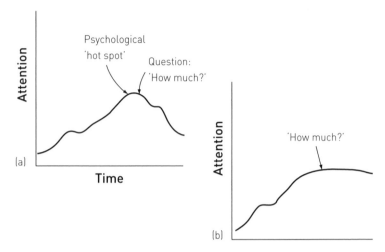

Figure 5.2 Maintaining attention by using memory at a crucial moment: (a) without memory, (b) using memory

'There seems something more strikingly incomprehensible in the powers, the failures, the inequalities of memory, than in any other of our intelligences.

The memory is sometimes so retentive, so serviceable, so obedient. At others, so bewildered and so weak – and at others again, so tyrannic and beyond control.'

Jane Austen (1775–1817) *Persuasion*

We've seen throughout this chapter how you can improve your memory in specific situations and how it can pay enormous dividends in your interpersonal dealings with people. It helps us to avoid rifts and misunderstandings in all our relationships, both in work and in life in general. More importantly, it helps to create **rapport** – a vital persuasion skill. **Sharpen your memory and you'll see the magic.**

Coffee break . . .

In business and personal life, the c_____ that comes from a good power of recall is invaluable.

Unlike short-term memory, long-term memory has no known limits. You can 'r_____' information in your short-term memory until it eventually becomes stored in your long-term memory.

Link new information to the 'self' and form a_____ for rapid recall.

Much 'forgetting' is actually an i_____ problem – the information was never picked up in the first place (you can't forget what you never knew!).

Remembering names is a powerful r_____ builder and is extremely persuasive.

In most cases it's because you're d_____ at the time of an introduction because your m_____ is elsewhere.

Beware of making e_____ p____ that you then forget and the other person remembers – trouble!

Good use of memory helps you to control a_____ when you're with other people (less eye-contact loss and break in dialogue while searching for information).

Remember: 'All k_____ is but remembrance' (Plato).

Chapter

'When *I* use a word,' Humpty Dumpty said, in rather a scornful tone, 'it means just what I choose it to mean – neither more nor less.'

'The question is,' said Alice, 'whether you *can* make words mean so many different things.'

'The question is,' said Humpty Dumpty, 'which is to be master – that's all.'

Lewis Carroll, *Through the Looking Glass*

Make words work for you – the power of psycholinguistics

Success can depend on saying the right thing at the right time

- Choose your words carefully
- Measure twice – cut once
- Assume makes an ASS of U and ME
- Questions, questions …
- Be careful with 'why?'
- Don't 'you' be negative
- Be persuasive with open communication
- It ain't what you say
- Men and women in conversation

Do you overlook the power of words in your dealings in everyday life? Are you aware how some words seem to 'work' and others don't? Do you choose your words carefully and monitor their effect? Not enough attention is paid to the subtleties of making effective word associations – considering the different outcomes that are possible when words and phrases are constructed and delivered in alternative ways.

Researchers in **psycholinguistics**, a branch of psychology devoted to the study of verbal behaviour, observe how we use language and how verbal abilities interact with other cognitive abilities – **how words affect our minds and emotions.**

Language can influence thought, and words are the tools we can use to create mental images. We're always reminded of how politicians use 'double-speak' – language that is used deliberately to confuse, mislead, conceal and distort meaning. An economic slump may be described as 'negative economic growth'.

Politicians and estate agents are likely bedfellows – they both suffer from similar image issues and regularly top the polls as the least trusted people. We all know how an estate agent's sought-after 'property of the week' (which was not selling) described as 'needing extensive updating and modernization' may suddenly reappear as 'refurbishment opportunity'. Words can be used to shape and, sometimes distort, the way that we think.

Think of the emotive term '**global warming**'. When it was first mooted there was a lot of fear and also widespread scepticism as to the validity of the claims made by scientists and politicians. Certain countries refused to open discussions about a theory that had insufficient proof to back-up its claims. What changed? The psycholinguistics changed.

There was a 'rebranding' to the more palatable '**climate change**'. The result? There has been more cooperation between governments and other agencies and a succession of summits addressing the possible problem.

The year 2009 threw up a whole host of terms to make society more accepting of unfavourable policies and situations. The previous year's disasters with the financial and banking system gave us the reassuring (and blameless!) term, '**credit-crunch**'. A handy term to use (and abuse) for all the ills that were facing us. An excuse for price rises in the shops; for poor service; for a general malaise. An inoffensive term for a serious situation that was facing some economies.

This led to the uncomfortable situation where the only option for some governments was to print more money. This was a very unpopular move in terms of public reaction. So in came '**quantitative easing**' (QE) to 'ease' the pain. The printing of money is achieved in an indirect way as – in the case of Britain – the Bank of England buys up gilts. One arm of the government is buying up gilts owned by another arm of the government in exchange for money created by the central bank. Is that printing money? The politicians' answer is 'No'. To any economist the answer is 'Yes'. A cartoon in one of the national newspapers caught the mood of a befuddled public. The character is saying: '*I now know what quantitative easing means. Trouble is, I don't know what money is anymore.*'

So much for that other word that has been flaunted by governments and other organizations: '**transparency**'. This was not very apparent in restoring faith in democracy when the MPs' expenses scandal broke in 2009. After exposure in the newspapers, the Commons – in crisis – agreed to release files of the individual MPs' expenses for publication in the national newspapers. What followed was the release of files with text relating to controversial claims heavily censored – unsightly blacked-out text on the pages. Public anger was refuelled.

What was the reason for the censored documents? Simple. Some information had been '**redacted**'. Redacted? *Oxford English Dictionaries* were being thumbed-through everywhere. Censoring or editing was the prevailing definition. But for this definition, it was bureaucrat-speak for drawing a black line through something. Draw your own conclusions. Oh, the power of words!

Think about it. You want to convey something to somebody. You have in your mind an **image** that you translate into **words**. You then, as the sender (encoder), transmit this **message** to the receiver (decoder). This person takes your words and translates them back into an **image** – their *own* image. They decide what it means. The interpretation takes place inside their mind.

If the other person's mental picture doesn't correspond to yours, then communication has not been effective. The word associations sparked off by your choice of words may produce a *negative* result.

How a person feels is determined by their interpretations. As human beings, we (in the following order):

1 sense

2 interpret

3 feel.

So, we are able to control what we feel by the simple act of changing our **interpretations** (the basis of much cognitive therapy); this changes our feelings. Not an easy task, but it can be done. So much of what we hear or read can be misinterpreted through bad choice of words. '*That's not what I meant*' is something that you're probably used to hearing in arguments at home and in other areas of your life.

Harriet (to John): 'Every time I look in the mirror all I can *see* is wrinkles. I look in the mirror and I see flabby arms. I see big hips. I see big thighs. I see cellulite everywhere. Oh, John – say something positive to give me hope.'

John: 'Errr . . . At least there's nothing wrong with your eyesight.'

Ouch! A good example of why it is necessary to go beyond or between words to search for the emotional content of any communication.

That is why it is so important to get feedback from the listener. Making verbal communication effective and clear involves both the sender of the message and the receiver.

Choose your words carefully

Consider the following examples, in which Amanda leaves a message on her friend Sally's answerphone. Which should she use?

1 'I won't be able to come to the Elvis Presley anniversary concert at the Royal Albert Hall on Saturday, Sally. You'll have to try and sell my ticket. I'll pay you if you can't. John's back and he's taking me out. Sorry about that. Talk to you soon. Bye.' (*Sally had queued to get the tickets weeks ago.*)

2 'Sally, isn't it great? John's been given a weekend off from his job in New York. He wants to take me out. Doesn't know when he'll get over again. So I can't make the concert on Saturday. I can understand if you're disappointed – I'm sorry, I was really looking forward to it. Perhaps you can try and sell the ticket. Otherwise don't worry, I'll pay you back. I hope we can arrange something else soon. Bye for now.'

Which one will be less of a blow to her friend? The message and request are essentially the same. But the first would leave Sally feeling a little rejected. Too much of 'me' and not enough concern for her. The second message starts off in an enthusiastic, positive way. Then it goes on to explain further and acknowledge Sally's possible feelings. A little thought on Amanda's part and the relationship will remain on a better footing. The first message has 49 words, the second 78. Hardly a great sacrifice in terms of *time*.

Of course, human nature being so complex, it's impossible to know exactly how particular words will be interpreted and thus received. **But if we can get inside the mind of the individual, we can choose the words that will have the best chance of achieving the desired effect**.

Measure twice – cut once

Another example: a human resources manager is standing in the corridor with the managing director. He says to a passing secretary: 'Have you seen Tom Collins? We need to discuss the training budget.'

'Yes,' replies the secretary. 'As a matter of fact, I saw him about ten minutes ago, tottering up the stairs towards accounts.'

It's now 2.30 p.m., so the HR manager assumes that Collins has been for a 'liquid lunch'. His mind has latched on to the word 'tottering', with all its implications. He has a mental image of Collins being below par, and he doesn't want to risk the MD seeing Collins in this state. He makes an excuse for deferring the meeting.

In fact, there are a number of possible explanations:

- The secretary may have used the word 'tottering' simply because it was the first one to come into her head. She had actually meant to say 'trotting', but it came out as 'tottering'. (Perhaps *she* had the liquid lunch!)
- Collins had been weight-training or playing squash during his lunch break, so he looked and felt tired.
- Collins was suffering from a bad attack of migraine.

However, the use of that one throw-away word introduced a *negative* association. The HR manager now sees Collins as someone who drinks too much at lunchtime. It is a mistaken impression, formed by a single word, but the idea has taken root. An assumption incorrectly brands somebody as a drunkard.

Let's take a further example. A solicitor is annoyed at the unusually poor quality of his secretary's typing. The number of serious mistakes is becoming intolerable.

He tells her: 'Sandra, your typing's very shoddy lately. It's important that the invoices are accurate when they go out. It's very difficult to get clients to pay up on any shortfall if it's due to our mistakes.'

The instant Sandra hears the word 'shoddy', her blood pressure rises and she becomes defensive. She's bitter at the personal affront.

'Doesn't he know,' she seethes, 'that those two extra staff transferred from the City are giving me lots of contracts to type? I'm snowed under! How am I supposed to cope? Doesn't he consider that? I only stay here out of a misguided sense of loyalty. He can keep his invoices. He can keep his job!'

The solicitor would probably still have Sandra on his payroll if his approach had been something like this:

'Sandra, your typing's not up to its usual impressive standard. Any problems?'

This is an *invitation* for the secretary to offer reasons, and she naturally wants to justify not reaching her normal 'impressive standard':

'Well, Mr Keen, I'm sorry if you think that. The truth is, I just can't cope. I don't know whether it's been brought to your attention, but the two gentlemen from the City office have been giving me at least six detailed contracts to type every day.'

'Oh, I didn't realize. If invoices go out with errors, it holds up payment. Also, it's difficult to get the clients to pay up if there's a shortfall due to our error. OK, I'll see if their typing can be done by Mrs . . .'

Net result: he's had a chance to compliment and criticize (nicely), and Sandra will strive to reach her former 'impressive standard'. (*Oh, and the solicitor **still** has a secretary.*)

Our woodwork teacher at school was always telling us to **'measure twice – cut once!'** as he collected up the abortive pieces of wood that we'd sawed without double-checking dimensions. So we'd have to go through the process again, when of course it could have been avoided.

Not a bad phrase to adopt when you're considering choice of words. Try to get it right the first time and momentarily double-check what's about to come out of your mouth, and so avoid all the aggravation and effort of *undoing* your previous verbal misdemeanours.

Measure twice – cut once! It's a little more difficult when dealing with people, as we're not just dealing with blocks of wood (well, sometimes we are!) but it can save an awful lot of misunderstanding and aggravation.

Assume makes an ASS of U and ME

Studying how words affect our minds and emotions is fascinating because we are constantly in communication with people: reading, writing, listening and speaking.

Surely a moment's thought as to how a word or phrase may be interpreted by another person is worth the effort?

The wrong choice of words has precipitated many wars, divorces, fights, arguments and business bust-ups. We make assumptions based on what people are saying or doing and quite often respond *before* testing the validity of our assumptions.

Hotel manager (to reception-desk staff): 'I don't believe it! You're not considering the guests, are you? There are enough of you in reception. I passed by in the lobby 20 minutes ago with the regional manager and we saw five people waiting to check in and an American couple who were waiting to check out. They didn't look too pleased. This can't carry on. With the new five-star opening around the corner next year, these people can go elsewhere. This is not Fawlty Towers. Why aren't you monitoring the queues? This just won't do.'

Well, the accusatory statements didn't allow for, or even encourage, any dialogue from the reception staff. They almost certainly encouraged *defensiveness* and *annoyance* on their part. Perhaps the reservations computer system was down and this caused a temporary build-up. They certainly weren't asked for an explanation before the outburst. The manager was more concerned that the guests, in the future, might 'go elsewhere'. But there's a distinct possibility that the staff may now decide to go elsewhere!

A more effective approach and use of words could have been:

'Just a quick word with you all. I noticed a lengthy queue here about 20 minutes ago. Was there some problem?'

'Yes, Mr Cleese. The computer went down for about five minutes. We were handling the paperwork manually during that time. We apologized to those in line, and Mark has arranged with room service for a complimentary drink to be taken to their rooms.'

'Oh, I see. Is the system running OK now?'

'Yes. It seems fine, but we've called the IT department just to take a look at it – they'll be here at two. We don't want it to happen again – don't want our clientele to be tempted by the new hotel down the road, do we? You know how some of our American guests wouldn't hesitate to "bust your ass" Mr Cleese.'

'Er . . . quite. Well done, Polly.'

Remember: we are all practitioners of persuasion, and our basic tools are words. But, like all good craftspeople, we have to know which are the *right* ones to select from the toolkit for the job in hand. It's usually laziness that prevents people from doing this. It's easier just to leave the brain in low gear and say:

'I <u>disagree</u> totally with what you're saying.'

'I'm <u>not happy</u> with your work.'

'I'm <u>afraid</u> we can't deliver for eight weeks.'

'I <u>regret</u> to inform you . . .'

'You <u>must</u> tell me how much you're paying at the moment if we're to . . .'

'<u>Bad news</u>. I've spoken to the engineer and the earliest he can come out is . . .'

People spend their time brainwashing others that **things are worse than they really are**. Why do they do it? They make it hard for themselves by creating bad feeling when there needn't be any. Get inside the mind. There are much better ways of phrasing the preceding statements. How about:

'Won't you look at it this way and imagine it from my point of view?'

'Any reason why we're getting more complaints for your section?'

'We'll get your jogging machine to you sometime within the next eight weeks.'

'We have to tell you . . .'

'It would be helpful if I knew how much . . .'

'The engineer's busy, but he knows it's important to you and he'll get out to you by . . .'

If you've ever played the word-association game, you'll know how your mind triggers off an image in the subconscious. It's quite automatic. A word evokes a certain feeling and a picture in the mind.

So make sure the message you're communicating is conveyed in the right words and also at the right time. Certain words may be appropriate at one time but not at another. You are then far more likely to get the result you are after.

We're talking not about deception, but about **perception**: using the right tools for the right job, and understanding the psycholinguistic connotations of saying things in certain ways.

Questions, questions . . .

The way we phrase questions to draw out information from other people is crucial. Questioning is an important skill that is needed in communicating successfully. There are **open** questions and there are **closed** questions.

The open question uses words in such a way that the respondent answers in more detail and at greater length. For example, if I said to you, 'Do you like horror films?' (closed question) your answer might be short and specific. 'What sort of films do you like?' (open question) would probably elicit a fuller, longer reply.

Open questions are useful for 'getting inside the mind', as they encourage self-disclosure. You can use them to find out a person's true, possibly hidden, motives or desires.

Closed questions, by contrast, will often generate a monosyllabic one-word reply like yes/no. They lead to a rapid ending of a conversation. For example:

'Do you like working as a PA?' (closed)

'What made you go into this line of work?' (open)

'How's life?' (closed)

'So, what's been happening lately?' (open)

Those good old indispensables *what?, when?, how?, where?* and *who?* are also good problem-solving tools. They too encourage people to reveal their innermost feelings. (There may be a general reluctance to use these old favourites for fear of appearing too forward. Correct delivery helps overcome this problem.)

'Can I ask *who* is likely to be involved in the decision?'

'*What* can we do to ensure that you don't have this problem again?'

'*When* is the ideal time for you to research the radio archives for me?'

'*Where* would you like to see yourself after two years?'

'*How* do you feel about the suggestions that were put forward?'

Like open questions, these are effective questions for getting inside the mind. But the way in which they are asked, and the rapport (or lack of it) that has already been established, will determine their effects. They will obviously be more successful if you have managed to strike up some empathy with the person you are dealing with.

Be careful with 'why?'

People often ask why we exclude *why?* from the list. The reason is that it requires a *rational* explanation for our behaviour. We often don't know why we do or did things. If asked, our inclination is to be defensive. 'Why?' makes us want to justify ourselves rather than look at possible alternatives for the future.

'Why' questions can be misinterpreted as accusatory, hostile, judgemental, or personal:

'*Why* did you buy that?'

'*Why* would you think I'd be interested in that?'

'*Why* can't you just telephone and find out, instead of . . .?'

How about:

'Maybe it would have been better to go for ...'

'It's not something that I have a great interest in ...'

'Perhaps you can call them instead of trudging all the way ...'

Also, the word is synonymous with criticism:

'*Why* did you take that road? It would have been much quicker to . . .'

'*Why* can't you be more careful when you . . . ?'

'*Why* is your desk always the untidiest in the whole department?'

> **Criticism and advice deter people from analysing the reasons for their behaviour.**

How about:

'It's a pity we didn't choose that parallel road . . .'

'Try to be more careful when you . . .'

'Please try to keep your desk tidy as there are visitors passing by all the time.'

Notice that the simple rephrasing of these three statements has taken the emotional intensity out of the situations (why, oh why didn't you think of that before?). We've gone from assailing the person's *character* to finding a *solution* to a problem.

Don't 'you' be negative

Research shows that the word '**you**' can be responsible for much negative communication. Used in an accusing way, it can completely alter the course of a conversation and evoke a hostile reaction in the recipient:

'You always have to have the last word, don't you?'

'You never ring when you say you're going to.'

'You ought to go out and find yourself a job.'

'You always let me down when there's an important meeting coming up.'

Far better to rephrase statements like these and alter the feelings that the other person experiences. Replace them with statements that are more *constructive* than destructive. Using a more open style of communication should encourage discussion too:

'It seems as though the last word generally comes from your direction.'

'I always seem to expect a call from you on a certain day and it never comes.'

'I think it might be a good time now to look for that job.'

'I need your cooperation when I've got important meetings.'

Notice how much less antagonistic this sounds and how the emphasis has shifted to 'I', making you more assertive. You're now much more likely to be listened to by the other person.

Be persuasive with open communication

As we have seen, the style of communication determines how we come across and whether we can bring people around to our way of thinking.

Much miscommunication, and therefore strained relationships, arises from people adopting a **closed** style of verbalizing as opposed to an open one. What do we mean by that?

'I don't see how we can share a flat with Sarah. I know you like her, but she's always overdrawn on her bank account. She's always late turning up for work. Could we trust her to do her share? Types like her you'd think we were supposed to feel sorry for. She should make the effort to . . .'

This closed statement delivered to Sue precludes any hope of a reasonable dialogue because of its finality and the language used, leaving little room for the possibility of a reasonable discussion. Many people communicate this way, using this kind of language, and it leads to a **negative** communication climate.

An **open** style would be something along these lines: 'I'm concerned about Sarah sharing our flat, Sue. I know you like her, but she's often overdrawn at the bank, and her timekeeping at work isn't so hot. How do you feel? Do you think we could trust her to do her share of cleaning?'

This open style promotes discussion, as there appears to be less rigidity in the statements and an opportunity for a degree of flexibility. It invites a **positive** response from Sue, who may even end up agreeing. People prefer to deal with others who speak in an open communication fashion: it leads to less offence, less frustration and less defensiveness. **It promotes a healthy relationship and encourages others to come around to your point of view**.

There are **three** closed styles of communication statements often to be found lurking in everyday life, both in and out of the workplace, and they do nothing to help your communication become persuasive. We'll take a look at them and see how they can be converted to open statements.

The definitive

You hear this all the time (and you do it yourself). For example:

'He's the worst boss I've ever had.'

'They do the best cappuccino in the country.'

'You've got to stay late or they won't notice you.'

'They're the worst rugby team ever.'

These definitive statements are used by all of us in everyday life; although they may appear harmless, the closed nature of the statements means that the opinions come across as *fact*. It is not the comments that are at fault: *it's how they are stated*, as a truth rather than as an opinion, that often makes people turn off and discourages discussion. If the subjects concerned are really important, you can see how it can fracture relationships.

The open style of removing definitive statements involves the use of 'I' statements (we discussed these earlier). You use the word 'I' at the beginning of a sentence or in a phrase within the sentence. Or you can use phrases that denote an 'I' meaning.

In the examples above, we would change these to:

'I feel that he's the worst boss I've ever had.'

'I think they do the best cappuccino in the country.'

'I feel you've got to stay late or they won't notice you.'

'In my opinion, they're the worst rugby team ever.'

So, keep a watchful eye and ear, censor your tendency for definitive statements and make them open, using 'I' statements. As a side benefit, using 'I' is an assertive method of speaking and empowers the speaker, encouraging people to be receptive to what you are saying.

Some examples of possible 'I' statements are:

- I would say . . .
- I think . . .
- I consider . . .
- I feel . . .
- I believe . . .
- I like . . .
- As far as I can see . . .
- As far as I'm concerned . . .
- In my opinion . . .
- It appears to me . . .

- It seems to me . . .
- In my way of thinking . . .

The exaggerated

This is another familiar way of using words for most of us. You know, words like: everyone – always – never – every – anything – only – everybody – all.

Sarah (to Richard): 'Everyone knows that you get only two great loves in your life.'

Richard: 'Everyone? *Who's everyone*? Where'd you get that from?'

Sarah: 'I read it in a magazine.'

Richard: 'What magazine? *Convenient Theories For You Monthly*?!'

These are words that completely distort statements and can cause a total communication block and friction between individuals. For example:

'You never take me out to dinner.'

'He's always late for meetings.'

'I can't say I learn anything from that teacher.'

'You take all the best canapés.'

'Everybody knows that we're the best in the business.'

'You're only civil to me when you need some rush typing done.'

'All builders are unreliable.'

'You make every day I spend here a misery.'

These types of statements are used by us *all* the time (whoops!) – or rather, much of the time – and they are usually used for their **dramatic** overtones rather than their accuracy. They can cause a lot of damage in our interpersonal dealings. If we're trying to win people over, for whatever reason, they certainly do not promote harmony and acquiescence.

More often than not, they are inaccurate statements. A person may have been late for meetings a few times, but it might not be *always*. A man may not have taken his partner out to dinner for a while, but *never* is a bit harsh. You might think your products are the best in the business (as may a few of your customers), but *everybody*? *All* builders are unreliable?

In some cases, these words may convey an *accurate* statement (a person could have been late six times for the six meetings you've had), but we tend to use them to make a point, and it can lead to the opposite effect. Of course, when we hear these statements in everyday life, a lot of it is harmless ('Did you see his last film? He's got *everything* a girl could ask for . . .') but because of the emotional nature of the messages they can lead to inadvertent problems.

The best way to modify these exaggerated utterances is to call upon our good friends, the 'I' statements, where needed and then add '**softeners**' to take the place of the exaggerated word. These are words such as: hardly ever, frequently, rarely, most, usually, in general and almost. See if you can conjure up some more.

So now let's take a look at the revised statements:

'You hardly ever take me out to dinner.'

'He's frequently late for meetings.'

'I rarely learn anything in that teacher's classes.'

'You take most of the best canapés.'

'In my opinion, we're the best in the business.'

'I feel you're civil to me usually when there's some rush typing to be done.'

'In general, builders are unreliable.'

'I feel you make almost every day I spend here a misery.'

So, less drama and some scope for conversation and – who knows? – even conciliatory outcomes. As we said earlier: measure twice – cut once.

The forcing

These are words and phrases of a commanding nature and are often accompanied with the dangerous (as discussed) *you*, which, as we noted earlier, encourages the respondent to behave in a **defensive** and, more often than not, **antagonistic** manner:

'You *must* telephone your grandmother.'

'He *has* to polish up his communication skills, or else.'

'You *ought* to telephone if you're staying late.'

'They *must* be more considerate in future.'

'You *should* go to the ball, Cinderella.'

These forcing-type statements are often conveyed in the definitive style as well – so you can have double trouble, turning them into even more of a closed statement. Let's transform the statements above into more acceptable ones:

'It would be good if you telephoned your grandmother.'

'I believe he'd benefit from polishing up his communication skills.'

'You may want to think about giving us a quick call if you're going to be late.'

'It would help us enormously if they were more considerate in future.'

'It would be a good idea if you went to the ball, Cinderella.' (Reader: we know better – but don't get involved!)

It ain't what you say

An advertising executive, Mr X, wanted to attend a six-day conference in Las Vegas. The conference fee and travel expenses would add up to quite an expensive trip. His boss, Mr Y, was the type who didn't like spending the company's money. (He had a sign above his desk that read: '*I have enough money to last me the rest of my life, unless, of course, I want to buy something.*')

If he authorized any expense, Mr Y would always want to see an immediate return. Furthermore, if people went on overseas trips, it had to be work, work, work all the way.

Mr X knew that the month of July (when the conference was being held) was a fairly slack time for the company and for himself. So the timing was good, in his eyes. He felt that he might overcome the cost objection by telling his boss that many of his counterparts in other advertising agencies would be there.

But he feared that one factor would kill his plan stone dead: Las Vegas. It was bound to conjure up a totally unsuitable image in the mind of his boss: *gambling, scantily clad showgirls, Caesars Palace* – anything but a serious conference. Las Vegas just happened to be the venue (although obviously it was part of the attraction of going). So, Mr X decided that when he went to sell the idea of the conference to his boss, he would choose his words carefully and focus attention on the convenient date in the calendar and would mention the country (USA) rather than the specific venue. This is how the meeting went:

'**Come in. Sit down.**'

'**Thanks. I'll get to the point quickly. I was wondering – July is quite slack here for us, and the ADM conference takes place then in America. I'd like to go. It would be useful for us to have representation there. A lot of blue-chip client companies might be there – good for contacts. A lot of agencies are sending at least one person.**'

'**Mmm . . . How much?**'

'**Well, delegate fee plus travel . . . Suppose three to three and a half thousand.**'

'**That's quite expensive. You say a lot of other agencies are sending somebody? Mmm . . . You know we're over on the T&E budget already?**'

'**Yes, I know. But I really feel this would be a good year to attend. There's a two-day seminar on . . .**'

'**Hey, I've got an idea. If you could use the parent company's apartment on Manhattan East Side . . . Yeah, that would cut down on accommodation costs.**'

'Oh – but that's in New York.'

'Well, that's where the conference is, isn't it? That's what you said.'

'No, I didn't.'

Interesting how *association* is already at work in Mr Y's mind. Mr X only mentioned 'America', but his boss's mind was racing away for a solution. He assumed the venue was New York and even accused Mr X of having said so!

'Well, where is it being held?'

Mr X thought he was cornered; it looked as though his cause was lost. Then he had a brainwave (psycholinguistic solution): 'Where is it? Oh – Nevada.'

'Nevada. Oh . . . yes, Nevada.' (Pause.) 'That's the West coast, isn't it? Er . . . do they have an airport there?'

'Oh yes. And domestic flights are cheap, too.'

'Well . . . Look, I've got a meeting in five minutes. That's OK then, but keep the costs down will you?'

'Thanks. I will.'

A happy ending.

Look at what happened, and the thinking behind the moves:

1 Mr X anticipated the *association* that the words 'Las Vegas' would conjure up in his boss's mind.

2 So he decided just to mention 'America'.

3 He came unstuck because his boss *imagined* he'd said 'New York'. (Many people have poor memories – remember? *Or did you forget that?*)

4 He had to say where the venue was now. So he said 'Nevada'. It was the truth. The conference *was* in Nevada.

This was perfectly all right. It was up to his boss if he wanted to know more. The point is that Mr X probably would not have been booking a plane ticket if he had mentioned Las Vegas.

He had to get inside the mind of his boss and anticipate his *interpretation* of the idea. Having got over this hurdle, he then emphasized that domestic flights were cheap. This was not too relevant, in the scheme of things, but it struck the final chord as far as his boss was concerned.

So, back to basics. Psychology has given us the label of 'psycholinguistics', but what we're talking about are things we should be aware of **every day**: how words affect our responses, and the selective, tactful use of words to *get the desired results*.

You could say that, in the above example, Mr X helped his boss to make a particular decision.

As stated already, we often want to be persuaded to take a particular course of action. We're looking for a good reason to do it and we just want someone to convince us. Their skilful use of words may tip the balance.

Men and women in conversation

Lady Astor: 'If I were your wife Winston, I would put poison in your tea.'
Winston Churchill: 'If I was your husband, I would drink it.'

(Winston Churchill and Lady Astor during an argumentative weekend at Blenheim Palace)

We've heard the stuff about men and women coming from different planets but that obscures the more fundamental point: men and women *think* differently. If both sexes can understand that their opposite numbers will therefore *communicate* differently, the world would most certainly be a better place. Better marriages, better parenting, better friendships, better work relationships, less conflict.

Whenever the topic of the different genders in conversation comes up in my workshops and seminars, a torrent of anecdotes and frustrations emanate from the group. Such are the pent-up feelings of both male and female members of the group. Being able to discuss foibles and concerns regarding the opposite sex in front of others seems to have a 'therapeutic' effect; but more importantly it shows how big the problem is.

It also shows that there is still a lack of **self-awareness** in many of us when we're talking to the opposite gender. *This leads to misunderstandings*. Every aspect of life suffers – domestic, personal and work (where many of us spend the majority of our waking hours).

It's often said that men and women can understand each other perfectly *except* when they're listening, talking, compromising and negotiating with each other!

What are the most common 'complaints'?

From the females:

- Men often talk to us as though they're talking to men.
- They don't listen.

From the males:

- Women often misunderstand and 'fly off the handle'.
- They talk too much.

So – some men don't listen and also may talk to the opposite gender without making allowances; and some women talk too much and may also misunderstand and occasionally explode.

These are perceptions, of course, just like everything else when we're talking about interpersonal relationships. **But like everything in life, it's not reality that's important, but how you perceive things**.

Well, if men and women are not *adjusting* their conversational style – when talking to the opposite gender – and there's misunderstanding in 'messages' that both sexes are receiving, is there any wonder that relationships in personal and working life are often in conflict?

Research continually shows that – in the main – when it comes to language, women have the edge over men.

They have been shown to *hear* and *process* verbal information better than men, and also possess a more varied vocabulary. When language tasks are performed involving men and women, most of the studies reveal that women outperform the opposite gender. Small wonder that some men say that women talk too much. The studies have shown that they're better at talking.

In the past there has been a tendency to shy away from any talk or acknowledgement of a difference between the sexes. Thankfully, more research into brain chemistry (since the 1990s) and open discussion has led to general agreement that there is a difference between the sexes when it comes to **communicating**; not that one is *right* or *wrong* or *superior* – just a *difference*. Men and women see the world through a different filter. Again, to stress – not that one is right or wrong; we're just different.

So, let's put away any thoughts about stereotyping; the idea is to *acknowledge* that there are differences – and accept that misunderstandings can occur – and analyse and then adapt the way that we talk to each other, so improving relationships and avoiding unnecessary conflict.

The problem seems to be that males and females insist – or want, or wish – that the two sexes should think the same and be alike. But, quite apart from any brain chemistry issues, a simple analysis of *how* men and women speak, proves beyond doubt that we:

- think in a different way;
- converse in a different way;
- attach importance to things in a different way.

It's been said that women engage in **rapport** talk while men converse in **report** talk.

Put simply, the idea is that the male style of report talk is usually concerned with displaying **knowledge** and **skill** through verbal performance.

The female style of rapport talk is designed to make a **connection**, with a give and take of similar stories. Empathy and support are often considerations during the interchange.

So, the research suggests that men use language for **self-display** and by contrast women use language to express **affiliation**.

These two telephone conversations illustrate the point:

Alice: 'Oh, Sue. It's Alice here. You sound harassed.'

Sue: 'Alice. I was going to call you this week. Harassed? Yes, I suppose. Car in for a service, supermarket, appointment at the bank. Then the doctor a couple of hours ago.'

Alice: 'Doctor? Is everything all right?'

Sue: 'Yeah ... just had to pick up a repeat prescription. That dragon – that new receptionist tried to make out I hadn't asked Dr Todd – I was sure she lost it ...'

Alice: 'Is she that one that divorced ...?'

Sue: 'Yes, that's her. Quite a scandal with that estate agent chap – they were caught using a client's house that was for sale ...'

Alice: 'That's right, another agent that had the property for sale walked in on them with a prospective buyer – they had to use the property particulars to – err – hide their particulars. Red faces all around. Ha!'

Sue: 'I don't know how she can show her face, after what she showed. People have got such short memories. I heard something else ... You'll never guess ... Oh, just a minute, I haven't even asked how you are!'

Alice: 'I'm fine. I was just ringing up to tell you ... Hey, I've got a better idea. Free for a coffee in town later this afternoon?'

Imagine a telephone conversation with their two respective husbands:

John: 'Oh, hi Simon. How's it going?'

Simon: 'Yeah, not bad. You?'

John: 'Yeah, good. Bit tired. New guys at work. Having to train them and stuff. Leaving the office late.'

Simon: 'Oh, right. I've got a bit of that at the moment – trying to get some synergy going between the departments.'

John: 'Right. Just wanted to touch base about the tiles. Spoke to Bill. He's included edging tiles and allowed 10 per cent differential – five millimetres or so.'

Simon: 'That's fine. Give me a bell when you get the amount and I'll send the money. Great. OK. Talk to you soon. Alice all right?'

John: 'Yeah, she's fine, thanks. Cheers. Bye.'

So if women tend to engage in **rapport** talk and men in **report** talk (like everything in life, there will always be exceptions), the knowledge of this should help both sexes to understand each other's style of communication.

More importantly, there are benefits in *both* styles of communication. There are times when women may be better served in various situations by adopting a more direct style with 'economy' of speech; equally men could learn from women and adopt a more 'expansive' style of conversation, when talking to the opposite sex – when the situation warrants it. Women may require more **detail** in some instances. One-word or short-phrase answers might not cut it, as it may do when talking to another man. Similarly, men may sometimes require **brevity** when the situation demands it.

An awareness of the *differences* between the way men and women communicate is a good starting point for harmony. Certainly, this would dramatically improve our domestic and working environments. In the workplace we're all assuming artificial 'roles' and in this environment of control and hierarchy, there is always the problem of misunderstanding and conflict – especially between the sexes.

The next step is to recognise the opportunities for *combining* aspects of the two styles – and improving our interactions – to produce more favourable outcomes both in our personal and working lives.

So, be aware that since men and women may look at the world through different 'filters', there will always be scope for misunderstanding and conflict with the utterance of a single word or phrase or the way in which a message is delivered. In this era of an acceptance of the importance of 'emotional intelligence', we can learn from each other and understand the respective styles of communicating; and adapt when necessary.

You have to use words to communicate. You may as well choose the best.

How different the impact of Shakespeare's well-known refrain would have been if it had been phrased in an alternative fashion. Would Hamlet's question be so memorable and oft-quoted all these years later if it had been put this way?

'I'm not quite sure whether to commit suicide or not.'

As opposed to the immortal line:

'To be, or not to be: that is the question...'

Coffee break . . .

Psycholinguistics is a branch of psychology that studies verbal behaviour and how certain words affect our m_____ and e_____.

Humans *sense*, *interpret* and then *feel*, and so we are able to control what we feel by changing our i_____; we interpret words in a certain way. So, a change of word in a certain instance leads to a *different* i_____ and therefore a *different* f_____.

We are all practitioners of persuasion, and our basic tools are words. It's up to us to choose the right words for the occasion, but it's usually l_____ that prevents us from doing so.

Be careful with the words 'you' and 'why' in your conversations. They are communication and persuasion killers. They encourage d_____ and antagonism.

Try to avoid a c_____ style of verbalizing and replace it with a open style.

Don't make life worse than it is with statements prefaced by things like 'I'm afraid', 'I regret to tell you', 'Unfortunately', 'I hate to disappoint', 'I disagree with' and so on. Engage in some word therapy, eliminate the n_____ and be upbeat.

Remember – we all have to use words to communicate; so why not choose the b____?

Chapter

7

'To improve communications, work not on the utterer, but the recipient.'

Peter Drucker

Telephone telepathy

Learn to use the telephone to your best advantage and read situations better

- It started with a call ...
- Cultivate a good telephone manner
- Pick the right approach
- Business calls
- Timing
- When the other person has company
- Introducing yourself on the phone
- Setting up a meeting
- Less is more
- Telephone telepathy in action

The fact that you can make a call from anywhere and at any time on your mobile phone has resulted in many of us not using the phone *as well* as we should. Likewise, the ease and convenience of email mean that many people do not use the phone *as often* as they should. Never underestimate the value or power of a well-thought-out phone call. It's usually the kick-off to your goal.

It started with a call . . .

It would not be overstating it to say that most things in life begin with a phone call.

The composer Sammy Cahn was famously asked about his method for composing some of his great songs. '*What comes first?*' he was asked. '*The lyrics or the music?*'

'*The phone call!*' he replied.

Because it conveys impressions, your 'telephone self' needs to be on top form. We're all quite different in our manner when telephoning friends, relatives and people we know fairly well. When we use the phone in a business context, we quite naturally observe a different code. Being effective in the workplace often demands good telephone skills.

There's an increasing tendency now to *substitute* emails for telephone calls. That's OK if it's a follow-up to things you've discussed in person or on the telephone, and it's relevant for ongoing communication. Also, emails may be practical when dealing with things of an impersonal and perhaps transient or short-term nature – horses for courses. **But there's an increasing tendency now for the substitution of email messages for the telephone in instances that demand (initially, at least) some kind of human contact**.

> **Think carefully before you hit the 'send' button on an email, because quite often messages need to be delivered by voice – in a face-to-face meeting or on the telephone. An email written in the wrong way (lack of warmth, for example) can destroy an important proposition, business relationship or lifelong friendship. Sometimes it pays to pick up the phone.**

If you're trying to bring someone round to your point of view or way of thinking, it's important to remember, for example, that emails don't 'smile' or exhibit any 'paralanguage' to enforce impressions – in the first instance – as the telephone allows you to do. And it's one-way traffic compared with a telephone call – *you don't pick up on the other person's often hidden reactions*.

So . . . when to use email and when to use the phone? The simple answer is to **put yourself in the other person's shoes**. What do you think the situation demands, taking into account the *other person's* interests as well as your own? Don't hide behind emails when a voice conversation may be needed to persuade or perhaps smooth things over in a relationship.

Certainly **the fact that we can ring somebody from a mobile phone from any place and at any time has led to a gung-ho approach** to the use of the telephone.

The Archbishop of Westminster, speaking in 2009 on the way that communication seems to be evolving (especially with younger people), expressed concern that there seemed to be too much use of texts and emails and that relationships have been weakened by the decline in face-to-face communication. This, he suggested, was 'dehumanising' society, as some people were losing the ability to build interpersonal communication. He further commented: *'We're losing social skills, the human interaction skills, how to read a person's mood, to read their body language, how to be patient until the moment is right to make or press a point.'*

A greater awareness is necessary if we are calling a person on *their* mobile phone. They're taking the call *anywhere* and at *any time*. What does that mean? It means that we should be more aware of the **situational** factors that may affect the call.

Can you really get your point across – and the person's undivided attention – while they're parked at a red traffic light? Or when they're in the middle of lunch? Or in a crowded train carriage? These situational factors affect the **outcome** of a telephone call. It's better to gauge the situation and decide whether to call back at another time. It depends on the purpose of the call. Awareness and intuition are key.

In the business world, used wisely the phone paves the way for successful meetings and may also avoid the necessity for long trips. For instance, if clients feel so comfortable and reassured in their dealings with you over the phone that they don't request a face-to-face meeting, then you're saving that most precious of commodities: time.

Have you ever come back from a meeting with somebody – a solicitor, a planning officer from the local council, a colleague based at another branch, a potential client, an existing client – and said to yourself: 'I could have done all that on the phone'? Three or four hours, or even a day or two, with travelling and an overnight stay somewhere, could possibly have been avoided by a telephone conversation. This goes on every day, everywhere, because in many cases **the person's telephone self is not persuasive enough**.

With the rising costs of key personnel, downsizing, petrol costs, environmental concerns about carbon footprints and general time constraints imposed on us all in the present day, the telephone has now become the backbone of many operations. If you can use it to the greatest effect then the dividends are indisputable.

Of course the telephone has its frustrations for all of us, particularly – in this technological age of automated systems – because of the increasing absence of human beings at the other end of the line. Just a disembodied voice instructing us:

'Press 1 if you would like to stay on hold while the music gets more annoying and "tinnier".'

'Press 2 if you'd like to be transferred to the wrong person.'

'Press 3 to hear these two options again.'

'Press 4 for a recording of "We're experiencing a high volume of calls today".'

'Press 5 if you'd like a recording of "Your call is very important to us".'

'Alternatively: Press 6 to be transferred to a rude operator.'

The curse of automated telephone systems! However, the telephone is such an important part of our lives that whenever we do get through to our intended target – in personal or working life – our telephone self needs to be effective if we're to achieve our desired outcomes.

'At the end of every year, I tend to add up the time that I've spent on hold on the telephone and I subtract it from my age. I don't count that time as really living. I spend more and more time on hold each year. By the time I die, I'm going to be quite young.'

Rita Rudner, comedian

Cultivate a good telephone manner

Problem: some people, including so-called 'professionals', just cannot communicate on the telephone. They seem to undergo a complete change of personality when confronted with a phone call. They become stilted, nervous, incomprehensible, brusque or even rude, coming across as plain 'hard-going'.

Clients and colleagues can also have bad telephone manners. This makes your job that much more difficult.

> **The problem with any telephone conversation is that you cannot see the person you're speaking to, and therefore you cannot observe their body language.**

Nor can you use facial expressions or body language to enforce your message. This means that you must make your **voice** work much harder than you would have to in a face-to-face situation.

How? By your *choice of words* and *tone of voice*. In other words, it's the **paralinguistics** (as discussed in Chapter 4) that become important when dealing with communication on the telephone. Your voice intonation becomes your greatest asset, and it's how you sound at the other end of the phone that determines the reaction and outcome.

Remember the 55/38/7 (page 60)?

The telephone provides no visual information for us to **convey** or **receive** a 'what you see' message (the 55 per cent) to aid us in transmitting or interpreting additional feeling to the spoken word. This lack of a visual medium also has the effect of making some people resistant to 'give up the floor', as they monopolise the talking, darting from one topic to another. **General rule of thumb – aim to talk half of the time**.

People forget that a lot of the words they use when speaking to somebody in person are subconsciously chosen to go with a *facial expression* or *gesture*, an accompaniment that gives added meaning to the words:

'You're such a know-all, aren't you?'

'Oh, I don't think I can possibly sign this.'

'How are the results of the advertising campaign?'

'Terrible!'

All of these remarks could be interpreted quite differently over the phone without the usual accompanying wink or grin to signal humour. Facial expressions can turn an apparent insult into a joke. Over the phone, the listener would have to be alert to voice inflections to establish whether a remark was teasing or serious.

The body helps the voice

The telephone is all about sound. It's the balance of 'percentage' numbers that exclude the visual: the 38 per cent of how you **sound** and the 7 per cent of what you say (**words**). With a lack of any visual feedback (for both of you) the words have to be less *ambiguous* and the tone and pace of your voice become ultra-important.

Take advantage of the fact that your **body** can aid you in the impression you want to convey through your voice.

How does the body help? Well, for example:

- If it's a *difficult* call and you can feel your tone changing to one that is at odds with your words (the tone is suggesting tense, angry, hesitant, suspicious or whatever) then lean back in your chair, loosen your shoulders and also loosen your lips (remember the smile?) and you'll notice a significant change.

- Want to convey an easy-going tone to a conversation? Do what some of the newscasters do at the beginning of their news bulletin on TV and lean against your desk (or kitchen table or whatever). Notice how your **emotional** state is transformed in all these instances.

- Equally, be conscious of your breath when talking on the phone. If you've just told your child off for spilling jam all over the sofa, or if you've just had an altercation with someone at work, you're likely to exhibit shallow breathing. *Not a good time to pick up a call or make one*. What impressions would be conveyed?

- Ever had to make an uncomfortable call to a relative, friend, someone at work, to an organization with a complaint? Of course you have. Possibly every day of your life! Again, **take advantage of the body**.

In this case, make this difficult call standing up. Observe how different you can sound when you're not sitting down (there's a *breathing* advantage for a start). You can convey your self-esteem by sounding more assertive, confident and forceful. Try it. I haven't come across anyone who hasn't noticed a difference – for the better – when they try this.

It feels unnatural to have to speak without using body language; that's why it's a lesson to watch experienced communicators conversing on the phone. They act naturally. You see them using facial expressions and gesticulating, just as if they were speaking with the other person face to face.

This puts *feeling* into the message, which is picked up at the other end of the line. Acting out a conversation gives you the illusion of actually being there. It therefore makes your words more effective. You're not hampered by speaking into a plastic handset, and the changes of facial expression automatically create the right voice pattern. Try it. Experiment: *try being angry over the phone with a big smile on your face*. Doesn't work, does it?

Exactly the same principles apply to training people to speak on the radio. Professional trainers will invariably tell candidates to make their voices 'smile' whenever appropriate in order to communicate enthusiasm or any other positive emotion. This gives colour and character to the unseen speaker's voice and makes the message more likely to be heard. In some organizations you'll see stickers attached to each phone with the message 'Put a smile in your voice'. That's proof enough that people need to pay more attention to their telephone technique.

It's the misguided fear of feeling and looking silly that generally inhibits people from smiling into a receiver. *So they hide behind a monotone*. People fail to understand that by using all the other means of expression, you enhance your tone of voice and thus your delivery. And telephone is all about voice.

Pick the right approach

More often than not we are talking to strangers on the telephone – people whom we've never met. **And, more than likely, we're asking them to do things for us**. So we have to sell ourselves:

- 'I know you've got a backlog of jobs, I understand that, but being without electricity, it's so frightening for my four-year-old – she believes in ghosts as well!'

- 'I really do need to speak to Mr Hyde this morning. Is there a chance you could try to contact him and get him to call me during the coffee break at his conference?'

- 'I'm more than aware that your time's at a premium this week, Miss Sloane, as you're just back from holiday, but I think you'll find our meeting very worthwhile if you could find 20 minutes or so on Friday morning.'

What we say and how we deliver it are the keys. The way we react to a request depends on the way in which it is made. Consider how the following approaches would affect you.

Telephoning a doctor's receptionist for a home visit:

1 'Hello. My son's not feeling too well – his throat's been awful the whole weekend. I'd like the doctor to come round this morning. Or I'll accept between 1.15 and 2 p.m. I've got to go to the shops after that.' (More or less a demand.)

2 'I know it's Monday morning and the surgery's probably very busy, but I really do need the doctor to come round as soon as possible.' (A concerned manner, conveying that I can see your point of view too.)

Chasing up an insurance claim:

1 'I want my storm-damage claim settled immediately. It's two weeks since I sent it in. I'm not impressed with your company at all.'

2 'It's two weeks since I sent my claim form in to you. I know there's been a bank holiday and you've probably got trillions of storm-damage claims, but this is really causing me problems. Could you settle it quickly?' (Delivered with feeling.)

It's obvious which approaches are going to get the best results over the telephone, isn't it? Of course, there will always be the exception – *when some village is missing an idiot!* and you happen, unfortunately, to locate them at the other end of your phone line.

Practically every day we find ourselves in the situation of having to ask something of somebody; so we have to sell them the idea of cooperating. In order to achieve the right response, your telephone self is the key.

Business calls

In the business world, you may need to telephone to:

- find out some information about an organization;
- find out the name of the person that you need to deal with;
- talk to this person;
- fix up a meeting (or, in many cases, conclude business).

From start to finish, the process has to be handled delicately. First, you're asking someone (a stranger) to give you information. Then you're asking to speak to the person who would be dealing with your proposition.

Your first phone encounter is often with the secretary of the decision-maker that you want to reach. The secretary, often very powerful as a 'screen', is subconsciously deciding how he or she feels about you. If your voice is pleasant and smiling, but not sycophantic, it may get you past the first hurdle. (There's no pretence involved in smiling. If you went to the person's office and saw the secretary, you'd certainly be pleasant and smile. You happen to be present *on the phone*. What's the difference?)

The problem: **there are too many people telephoning this busy individual, trying to interest them in propositions**. And many of these people are bad news. They're just not professional in their approach. Result: decision-makers develop

a cocoon around them. You can rarely get through to them directly. Their mentality becomes like that of Dorothy Parker, the American humorous writer and critic, who remarked that whenever she heard the tinkling of her phone, her first thoughts were always '*What fresh hell is this?*'

So now these people are invariably 'in a meeting', according to their protective secretaries, who request you write in or fax or email.

The average stress-laden person in business is constantly fighting against time. There aren't enough working hours in the day to deal with internal meetings, look at memos, read emails, sort out personnel problems, read trade magazines, make out-of-town or overseas visits and meet visitors. Time is at a premium. So if you manage to get connected to the person, your story had better be good.

Take the process of making a telephone approach step by step. Your aims are to gauge whether the organization may be interested in your proposition; to find out whose 'domain' it falls into; and to be put through to that person if they are there. The stages are:

1 Contact with the switchboard operator or telephone receptionist.

2 Transfer to the relevant person/decision-maker's secretary, or someone else in the department.

If the first two steps are effective, continue through to:

3 Conversation with the decision-maker.

4 The next appropriate step, e.g. arranging a meeting with him or her.

This scenario is the pattern *most* business relationships usually follow at the start. So each step is crucial as a means to the end. If there is ineffective handling of the situation at any one stage, the whole thing collapses like a house of cards.

In general, you don't get a second chance to make a first impression!

These principles apply not only in face-to-face situations but even more so over the telephone. Your efforts don't begin at stage 3; they start right from stage 1. After that hurdle, the process begins. Now we'll look at the stages in detail.

First point of contact

'The travel manager is Mr Jenkins,' the operator tells you.

So you've found out who the travel manager is – but you still have to get past his secretary:

'Could I speak to him please?'

'All calls go through to his assistant first.'

'Oh. Could you tell me his or her name please?'

'Yes, it's Sylvia.' (*So irritating!* **With some calls, you'll get a first name of an individual, which is not very helpful for you. You can hardly say, when you're put through, 'Oh, hello Sylvia. Is it possible . . . ?')**

'Would you know her second name?'

'Yes. Trench – Sylvia Trench.'

Now you're through to the assistant.

'Mr Jenkins' office. Good afternoon.'

'Would that be Sylvia Trench?'

'Yes, speaking.'

It's back to the rewards of having the *courtesy* to remember people's names. You're appealing to the ego. Most secretaries regard themselves as personal assistants to their bosses. Many have just such a title. Switchboard operators and receptionists (especially if they're temps or new to the job) may be unaware of this. Don't do what almost everyone else does and refer to him or her directly as a secretary. The connotations of this for a real PA with a key role will not endear you to them.

Address them as a person in their own right – with a name. You've caught their attention, and psychologically they're predisposed towards you. You've confirmed their identity in the hierarchy, something people strive for in the office jungle every day.

Now for the difficult part. You've confirmed their identity. Next, try to establish *yours*.

It's at this stage that things either progress or fall apart. The trouble is that some individuals who screen calls for a busy boss take things too far. Their overprotectiveness can mean that their bosses don't get to hear about something that could be of interest. You have to increase your efforts to ensure that you get a hearing.

There are certain prerequisites, such as courtesy. There's no substitute. We like talking to personable, well-mannered people; there's a shortage, so if you exhibit courtesy you're halfway there. Most people are too lazy and can't be bothered. The next issue is: do you sound important? (All right, you *are* important, but that's not the point – do you *sound* important?) That's all the screener has got to go by. They can't assess your outward appearance on the telephone: you're judged on how you sound, what you say and how you say it.

Let's continue. You've just asked if Mr Jenkins is free:

'Could you tell me what it's in connection with?'

'Yes, of course. It's MBI International . . . My name's Case. I have to discuss a conference package with him.'

'Has he spoken to you before, Mr Case?'

'No, we haven't spoken yet.'

'I'll see if he's free.'

(After two minutes) 'He's rather tied up at the moment. Could you write in, perhaps?'

'It's not that simple. I need to actually discuss something with him, Miss Trench; I don't mind holding on. I only need four or five minutes of his time.'

'Just a moment, Mr Case.'

'Jenkins speaking.'

She's let you through the filter. Well done. But don't forget that bosses themselves can also relish playing hard to get. They feel powerful when they refuse to take calls. It gives them a sense of satisfaction. ('People want to talk to me, but I just haven't got the time' – **self-esteem boost**.)

They also think it necessary to keep impressing upon their secretaries that they're not prepared to talk to all and sundry. However, there's no denying the fact that assistants wield great influence.

Look at it from their point of view. They don't want to look inefficient to their boss; they have to be selective about who is allowed access. In reality, some carry this too far, so it's up to the caller to create the right impression and then to persist – pleasantly.

A boss may ask their secretary for a thumbnail evaluation (30 seconds) of the intruder on the phone and what the call is about. Then it's up to the secretary to *persuade* their boss to talk to you. ('He seems very nice, Mr Jenkins. It might be worth having a quick word with him.')

Chatting up your contact

When you eventually get through to the person you're aiming for, you are effectively a *guest* on their telephone line; you should conduct your conversation with that in mind.

You've certainly interrupted this individual in the middle of something. You don't know what kind of mood they're in. They could be at the height of a crisis. They may have just come back from an overseas trip that morning. They could be recovering from an illness. Their roof at home might have blown off in a gale. They might be in the middle of a meeting. But whatever it is, you can be sure they won't tell you. It's up to you now. **Use some of that ESP**. Where's your empathy – the quality most people are short of? Get inside the mind.

'Mr Jenkins – thank you for your time. I'll be brief.'

Two Brownie points. You've acknowledged that they're busy. That's courteous. Second, you've made a positive move towards ensuring that you get their attention while you're talking. You've promised to be brief. Music to their ears!

You know how it is. Somebody that you already know comes on the line. You've got a million things to do. If you know that person is inclined to go on and on, your mind says: 'Oh no, not him again.' Consequently you switch off, and all the time the caller is speaking you're *distracted* because you're trying to work out which sentence will be the last. **So you miss most of what's being said**.

So often, people take a phone call from a caller under sufferance, either because they find it difficult to say no or because they've refused many times before and they feel that they ought to put the person off for good. A negative situation from the outset, it starts to resemble a fencing match.

But when the caller says 'I'll be brief', the other person is more likely to drop their guard. They can afford to pay attention and listen. They relax a little and actually hear what's being said.

Certain types of people prefer you to get to the point quickly. Their own minds race away with what's being discussed, and it's no good you being left on the starting block. (**This type of person will feature in Chapter 9**.)

Many people prolong a telephone call by speaking in a slow monotone, throwing out sentences and failing to finish them because they've thought of something else. Their conversations, or monologues, go something like this: 'Maybe we can try and . . . I mean, if you're able to contract to a minimum of . . . Or I suppose I could see what I could do . . .' And it goes on and on. There's no beginning, no end – *no result*.

You may get away with this in a face-to-face situation where you may be seen to have compensatory qualities. But, of course, on the phone you rely solely on the projection of your message.

Ask yourself: 'What's *happening* on the other end of the line?'

Arranging a meeting

Situation 1

'Good morning. Advertising Solutions. How can I help you?'

'Good morning. Could you tell me who's handling conferences now?'

'I'm not sure. I'm a temp here. I'll see if I can find out . . . Just a moment . . . let's have a l-o-o-k at t-h-i-s list . . . Oh, I'll just take this other call . . . Now, where . . . conf- . Just a moment . . . Sorry, I'm back. Could you hold on a minute?'

'Yes.'

After three minutes of piped music and a 'your call is important to us' recording:

'I've been through to Customer Service. They said it depends.'

'Depends on what?'

'Oh, I don't know really.'

'Look, just put me through to them.'

'Hold on.'

Two minutes later:

'I've spoken to them again. They said they think it would be Mr Steed. I'll connect you to his secretary. I'm not sure whether she's in yet.' (Click)

'Steed speaking.' (Hurried and impatient voice) ☹

'Ah, Mr Steed. I'm through to you. Anthony Bates of Top Notch Hotels here. We've got a new five-star property with wonderful conference facilities. We've had lots of interest from companies like yours that arrange film screenings and celebrity dinners. I'd like to come and see you. Now, would Tuesday at 9.15 be OK, or would Thursday at 2.30 suit you better?' ☹

'Well – neither, really.'

'Sorry – what do you mean?'

'Well, Mr Notch, what is it exactly you wanted to talk to me about?'

'As I said, our new hotel.'

'What's the company again, Mr Notch?'

'It's Top Notch Hotels. Actually my name's Bates – Anthony Bates.'

'Right. Sorry, Mr . . . er . . . Bates. I'm in the middle of a meeting right now. My secretary's not in yet. Give me your number.'

'My number . . . Er . . . It's . . .' ☹

'I'll call you back in about 15 minutes. Goodbye, Mr Notch.'

Two hours later, and still no call.

Situation 2

'Good morning. Advertising Solutions. How can I help you?'

'Morning. You could help me by telling me who handles conferences these days.'

'I'll just check for you. Could you hold for a moment?'

'Certainly. Thank you.'

'I've spoken to Customer Services. They said it depends on what it's to do with.'

'Right. I understand. Could you put me through to them, please? It's probably easier that way.'

'Yes. Who shall I say is calling?'

'My name's Bates.'

'Trying to connect you, Mr Bates.'

'Customer Services, Emma Peel speaking. Is that Mr Bates?'

'Yes. Good morning. I just need to know who's now responsible for organizing conferences.'

'Certainly. That's Mr Steed. Is there anything I could help with?'

'Well, I'd like to have a brief word with Mr Steed, if he's available, about our new hotel; I'm only over for a short time as I'm based at our head office in Monte Carlo.' ☺

'Would you like me to put you through to his secretary?'

'That would be good, Ms Peel. Thank you.'

'Let me see if she's there.' (Click) 'Mr Bates, she doesn't seem to be answering. I'll put you through directly to Mr Steed's extension.'

'Steed speaking.'

'Mr Steed. I've just been speaking to Ms Peel – she's just transferred me to you. My company's Top Notch Hotels.' (Pause) 'My name's Bates – Anthony Bates.' (Pause) 'Is it convenient to talk?'☺

'Well, actually I'm with somebody at the moment. But go ahead. What's it about?'

'Oh – I've called at an inconvenient time. Can I call you later, when you're free? I'd rather do that.' ☺

'Very well. I should be free at around 11.30.'

'OK. I'll call then.'

'Sorry, what was your name again?'

'The company's Top Notch Hotels. My name's Bates.'

'Right. I'll speak to you later, Mr Bates.'

'Bye.'

At 11.35:

'Mr Steed. It's Anthony Bates here. I called you an hour ago.'

'Yes, Mr Bates. Top Notch Hotels, isn't it? What can I do for you?' ☺

'Well, we have a new five-star hotel in Cannes. Is that the type of property that might be of interest?'

'We use all types of hotels, for clients as well as our own staff. Just one example, at the moment we're doing something in Switzerland – in St. Moritz. We chose a hotel that was both welcoming and elegant. Well-established and well-regarded. Facilities are good. It's got a great health spa with a luxury indoor pool – always a plus. No wonder some of our people have stayed on at the hotel over the weekend – mixing pleasure with business – or is it the other way round, Mr Bates?'

'Ha – I couldn't possibly comment.'

'When did you want to come to see me? I'm up to my eyes in it this week, really.'

'Well, to be specific, as I'm only over for a few days, I wondered whether there might be a chance of, say, Tuesday at around 9.15? Or, if that's awkward, Thursday afternoon?'

'Thursday would be better. Would 2.30 be OK?'

'Yes. Can we make it 2.30 to 2.45, just in case I have parking problems?'

'That's fine. But you can use our car park at the back. Just give my name.'

'Thank you. See you then.'

'Goodbye, Mr Bates.'

At the other end of the line

You know how it is. It happens to most of us a lot of the time. The film that you haven't seen for ages is on television. You're absorbed – memories come flooding back. (*Oh yes – that laser – I remember. Mmm . . . how the hell did he get out of that?*

'*. . . D'you expect me to talk Goldfinger?*' '*No – Mister Bond. I e-x-p-e-c-t you to die! . . .*')

The telephone rings. You grab the remote and turn down the volume on the TV set. Cursing the interruption, you force yourself to the phone and snap out a 'Hello'.

'Oh, is that you, John? It's Tom here.'

'Tom – hi.'

'You sounded different. Anyway, listen. I had to ring you. Remember we were talking about that hotel in Venice last month? . . . Oh, just a minute John. Get away, Samantha – Daddy's on the phone. Go and help Mummy move your toys. No, you can't . . . Sorry John – *interruptions* all the time. Now, where was I? How's things with you both anyway? OK?'

'Yeah, yeah. Er . . . not bad.' (Mega-brusque.)

'Can you remember the name of that hotel, then, John?'

'What hotel?' (Glancing at the silent TV set.)

'The hotel in Venice. The one facing the canal.'

The conversation continues in the same vein.

This kind of situation occurs every day, at home and in the office. Can you imagine Tom, after the call, when his wife asks him, 'Well, how was John? Did he remember the name of the hotel?'

'Mmm – he was a bit strange.'

'Oh. What d'you mean by "strange"?'

'Well, he was a bit brusque, not his usual pleasant self.'

'You don't think Joanna's left him?'

'No, no.'

'Maybe we've upset him. You don't owe him any money, do you? Or have we borrowed something that we haven't returned? Maybe he didn't like his birthday present – I thought it was quite appropriate.'

'No, no. I don't think it's anything like that. Anyway, he definitely was a bit odd. He didn't seem to be paying attention to what I was saying. Just wasn't interested.'

'Well, maybe they had company – people round there. Did you ask him?'

'No, I didn't. Suppose I should have. Hey – you know, you could be right. Just before he hung up he was mumbling something about a *"Pussy Galore"*!'

What a situation! Both parties are left feeling disturbed by the call. Tom is cursing John for making him miss the important bit of *Goldfinger*, and Tom is inwardly annoyed with John. (*'Well, if he can't be half decent when I call him for a friendly chat – even if he did have company – he can forget it.'*) Later on, when the film is over, John may analyse the telephone conversation (what conversation?) and think to himself: *'Mmm, maybe I was a bit short with Tom. No – he wouldn't have taken offence.'*

The problem is very simple: when you telephone somebody, at work or home, you are bound to be *interrupting* them as they are gardening, writing a report, surfing the Internet, eating a meal, having an argument, in a meeting, in a crisis situation, watching television . . . But some interruptions are much worse than others.

Just imagine if Tom had used his head to get inside John's mind – and been more empathetic – once he'd picked up on his rather curt and spontaneous greeting:

'John, it's Tom here. Am I interrupting something? Can you talk?'

'Well, it's OK – I was just watching *Goldfinger*. Years since I've seen it.'

'I haven't seen that one. I was never into all that. Those Martinis – shaken instead of stirred – frightening! Hey, listen, I'll call you back at ten. It's not life or death. I'll talk to you later.'

'But . . .'

'No, don't worry. Talk to you at ten. Bye for now.'

What a different scenario to the previous one. John is impressed by Tom showing such empathy. It doesn't fail to register. And he'll almost certainly be the one to make the call at 10 p.m., before Tom does. And he'll be all ears too.

People don't concentrate on what you're saying if their minds are elsewhere. You're being two-timed again. It can't be repeated often enough. The effectiveness of your message over the phone will be at its optimum only if the other party is paying full attention.

> **Most people don't let on that you're interrupting them or that you've caught them at a bad time.**

It's up to you to detect it from their tone of voice – remember, telephone is all about voice – and then decide what to do. *You* must take the lead; it's in *your* interest.

Timing

If you catch a person at the wrong time, it could be the *end* of your relationship, your sale, your pay rise, your request for an urgent call-out to the plumber, your trip to a trade fair, your request to have a day off. **And you usually don't get a second chance**. Remember the point made earlier: people generally don't like to change their minds after refusing a request. It makes them look indecisive and appear as though they made a mistake in the first instance (ego again). Even if they know that they were wrong, they may stick rigidly to their original decision, which may have been made hastily.

Why was it made in haste? Because they were *busy* and wanted to get rid of you. If you had picked up the vibes and offered to call back . . . *different story perhaps*. Let's face it, sometimes it's easier in life to say no immediately, if you're pushed for time and preoccupied.

So **timing** is all important. If you can tell from a person's strained voice that it's not a convenient time, and therefore unconducive to your cause, *nip the conversation in the bud*. Sometimes the other party does it but in most instances it will have to be *you*. **You may have more to lose**.

This point is so important (and so neglected) that it deserves repetition: knowing *when* and *when not* to speak to somebody on the telephone can make the difference between moving mountains and molehills. Be aware of the **situational** aspect at all times. It's usually make or break.

When the other person has company

Quite often when you call someone in an office, they are with another. They may tell you this and suggest that one of you rings back later:

> 'I'm in the middle of a meeting at the moment. Can I call you back?'
>
> 'I have someone with me. Can you call back later?'

If, as in the first example, they offer to ring you back, say that you will call. It's better that way. They are quite likely to forget.

You will save yourself waiting and wondering. Even if they haven't forgotten, your call may now be low priority (with all the problems that have emerged from the meeting you interrupted). It's at basement level in their in-tray.

If the other person tells you that they are with someone, you're lucky. More often than not you won't be told. **That's where the trouble starts**.

Problem: *people talk differently on the phone when someone is with them*. The reasons include:

- they are nervous;
- they want to impress the person who is with them;
- they're conscious that they're keeping the person with them waiting (and therefore hurry the conversation);
- they don't want the person present to know about the topic being discussed;
- they're speaking through an intercom phone, and their audience can hear your every word.

Catch yourself when you are alone, talking in the privacy of your own home or office. Your telephone conversation is probably quite fluent, as you gaze at your familiar surroundings. You don't have to watch what you say at your end. Nobody can hear you. It's a private conversation between two people.

Now compare this situation with one in which you are with another person or a group of people. You may adopt a more officious tone; you may be less friendly, less 'playful' even. Your words are chosen more carefully, so you become *less natural* and *less fluent*. You're conscious that your dialogue is being 'vetted' by the other person present. It's natural.

If you are phoning somebody for the first time to try to gain their interest, and they happen to have somebody with them, you could have problems. They may be the type that's always ready to impress the person present. It could be their boss who is with them. So they may try to 'kick you around'. It's done for show. Their audience see a bravado display that says: 'I know how to handle potential time-wasters. My time is important.'

You may be a nice person. Your telephone manner may be excellent, your proposition wonderful. But there'll be an artificial rejection of your call because the other person wants to look clever and powerful in front of their onlookers.

If they're having a meeting of some sort, a phone call forces a break in the proceedings. Meetings have various levels of importance. Their secretary, partners, chairperson, advertising agency or liquidator could be in the office. It would be fine if they told you to call back. *But many people don't*, often because they think it will be an inconvenience to them (or to you).

If they do take your call then their *concentration is wavering* because they're aware of keeping the people in their office waiting. Their time is valuable too. The easiest way to get you off the line is to say no to your proposal, regardless of its merit.

Sometimes, your call may be a confidential follow-up to something you've already discussed. They don't want the person present to know that they're thinking of buying a cottage in the Dordogne, or purchasing an office jacuzzi, or considering hiring consultants for a project. Their conversation with you thus becomes stilted and monosyllabic, and you think they're no longer interested.

It's important to bear in mind that if the person you're calling has company then you have to work hard **to read their tone of voice**. This will give you a pointer as to whether you should risk a quick shot at your request or proposition, or whether you should wait for a more favourable opportunity.

If you're speaking to somebody for the first time, it's as well to ask if *it's convenient to talk*. Even if you've passed through the 'filter' and they have agreed to speak, this gesture can make the person more responsive.

> **The golden rule is: assess whether the time is right to make your request or put forward your proposition, or whether you would get a better hearing at some other time.**

How many times have you come off the phone and thought to yourself: 'That's strange. He was interested when we met last week; what could have happened? He sounded completely different, tense almost'? (And how many times have people thought that about you?)

The person probably sounded different and less receptive because they weren't alone. You should assess the situation and cut it short. If you go ahead regardless and risk having your say, perhaps when telephoning someone for the first time, then if it's the wrong moment you may lose out and never have another opportunity.

The moral: if you're in any doubt, ask whether you're interrupting something. You're getting inside the mind. You're showing your powers of ESP (Empathy + Sincerity = Persuasion).

Timing is vital if we're trying to be persuasive in a situation. We will often respond to the same approach completely differently at different times; it's human nature. Sometimes the reason is **cognitive** (mood), sometimes it's **circumstance**. It should be stressed again and again: bringing something up at the wrong time can lay it to rest for ever. Waiting until the right opportunity can lead you straight to your goal.

You know all about timing in your home life. You'll wait until the time is right before you bring up anything important:

'Darling, sit down. Shall I get you a glass of Chardonnay? There you are. How was the meeting today? It went well! I'm so glad. The prospect of a salary increase from next month? That's wonderful news . . . Another glass? There you are. You know you said you were going to take time off in September? Well, Emily showed me this Mediterranean cruise offer that was in the *Daily Mail*.'

In the working world, much potential business is lost because the caller cannot understand the need to be **intuitive** before pitching on the phone. Would you ring a potential client at 9.15 on their first morning back from a two-week summer holiday to talk about something you discussed almost on the eve of their departure? Would you call your boss, the managing director, about your adventurous choice of a new company car on the morning that they discover that the company is the subject of an unwelcome takeover bid?

People generally respond better if they're in a good mood and not under pressure, and when things are going fairly well. Show some perspicacity. **Time your requests to your advantage**. In other words, call when the other person is able to give their best attention. Good thinking is essential in personal relationships, and it's crucial in the business world. We should constantly be aware of this. We know it's true.

Introducing yourself on the phone

Back to our telephone encounter.

You've got through to Mr Jenkins. So take things one step at a time. You know that using his name will make the whole approach more personal. You want him to remember your name, and your company's name – or, at worst, one of the two. Research has shown that most people contacted by phone are more concerned about missing the company name than that of the caller. They don't mind asking for your name at the end of the call (if they've got empathy, and can be bothered, they'll want to know your name at the outset so they can be courteous and address you by it).

The problem: on getting through to Mr Right, most people blurt out both names in one elongated phrase (often mumbled): 'Hello, it's Justin Case of MBI International here. I wondered if we might meet to discuss . . .' (no pause for breath). Sometimes, almost as if they are ashamed, people feel obliged to speak as fast as possible – to get the petty details out of the way. Petty? Your name, the company's name? Hardly.

Just a reminder. We live in a world in which we spend most of our income on '**wants**' rather than '**needs**'. We usually have to be informed about those products and services that we later designate as 'wants' – a superior overhead projector, an infrared night torch, a new breakfast cereal, sponsorship of a sporting event, etc.

When you're calling a potential client or whoever, you may have a product, service or proposition that could be a real asset to them – and their organization (in that order). There's no room for lack of self-esteem. If it sounds interesting, they would often prefer that you justified their time (and your own) spent speaking on the phone and fix up a meeting. After all, nobody likes to miss out. You might have some interesting ideas.

So when you introduce yourself by phone to a stranger, **be aware of how much their mind can take in at once**. You want your identity firmly established. So say it *slowly*: 'Mr Jenkins. Good morning.' Pause. 'It's MBI International here.' Pause again. Let him assimilate and remember. Let his mental computer do a rapid search for recognition. Now that the first bit has sunk in, you can state your name: 'My name's Justin Case.'

Think about it. You give the person a chance to either recall or register the name of your company. Then you give them the opportunity to hear your name and therefore remember it. Result: they don't feel as if they're talking to just a voice. That's better for you, because:

- it's easy to reject a *voice*;
- it's harder to reject a *person*.

Just think of a call you've had from somebody who rattled off their name and organization. If you're preoccupied, you may have missed both pieces of information. You don't feel any *rapport* with the person speaking and, as you're busy anyway, the inclination is: 'How do I get this **voice** off my line?'

To recap. You've said you'll be brief; Mr Jenkins has computed that. You've given the name of your organization; he's computed that. And then your name; hopefully he'll remember it, but if not, it's easy for him to say, later on in the conversation: 'I'm sorry, I didn't catch the name.'

There's every chance too that if you enunciate clearly and pace your words, then the listener will feel like writing down these important details while you're passing them on.

Setting up a meeting

Right. You've sorted out the identity problem. Now you want to see if you can arouse interest in your services and perhaps arrange a meeting. But remember that before people will agree to see you, they want to be reasonably sure about some key points:

- That they like the sound of *you* – and therefore of what you stand for.

- That your product or service *shows promise*, so they're not wasting time that could be better spent on a pressing report, in an important meeting, on the golf course, or whatever. There is sacrifice involved, after all.

- That you would be easy to *get rid of* if there is no common ground. This is a very important consideration and it cannot be stressed too much. Many meetings never happen because of a pushy attitude over the phone. The person thinks: 'If I can't get this person off the phone, what would they be like once they'd infiltrated my office (or home)?' So, although they may well be interested, they are put off the whole idea.

Nobody really likes saying no – especially in person. *It's easier on the telephone*; one can fence and say, 'Send me some literature', and end the matter there. When telephoned again, the secretary can say that their boss has looked at it, that they're not interested 'at the moment' but that 'We'll put it on file and . . .'; the equivalent of Hollywood's 'Don't call us – we'll call you'.

Because the other person needs to feel comfortable about being able to say no after a face-to-face meeting, **how you come across on the phone determines whether they agree to meet you**. If you show that you're willing to invest time then you've got a good chance.

Yet so many people fail to get that all-important first meeting because they cannot see the psychological reasoning behind this. They mistake aggression for confidence. There's nothing wrong with being confident about your services; in fact, it's a prerequisite. But there's a thin line between just enough confidence and too much.

They also mistake enthusiasm for confidence. Again, there's nothing wrong with being enthusiastic, but some people go over the top. It gives the whole conversation an air of falsity. It puts the other person off. They end up refusing to see you.

They're thinking: 'I wouldn't mind knowing about this service – could be useful, especially as we're reviewing the people we use at the moment, since they let us down recently. But this person's irritating. I'll never get rid of them if I see them; they'll hound me.' *It's the caller's attitude that's to blame.* They didn't sell themselves well. Did the caller get inside the mind? No. The person refused to meet them for a negative reason. And that's tragic.

Less is more

Being told at the beginning of the telephone call that it would be brief made Mr Jenkins relax. How about using the same tactic when trying to arrange your meeting?

'I understand, Mr Jenkins, that you're involved in the arrangements for your company's fiftieth anniversary celebrations?'

'Yes, I am.'

'I've a feeling I might have met you at a seminar about a year or so ago, if my memory for names is accurate.'

'MBI, did you say?'

'Yes.'

'Could it have been at a conference in Vienna?'

'Yes, I think it was. I was convinced your name sounded familiar. Small world!'

'Isn't it? It's coming back to me now. We were staying in the same hotel, if I recall. It was right in the city centre – in the oldest part. Lovely frontage, I remember. Just at the back of the opera. Of course – a great hotel. My wife was with me – thoroughly enjoyed it. We also did the one day tour around the city. In fact the conference was worthwhile too!'

'Good to hear it. I certainly enjoyed the seminar. Now, I'm calling because I'd like to fix up a short meeting, half an hour or so. Ideally, within the next two weeks.'

'Well, this week's bad. Next week . . . Let me see – any time except Tuesday afternoon and Thursday morning.'

'OK. How about Monday, three o'clock?'

'That's fine. I'm writing it in my diary now. MBI . . . Mr . . . ?'

'Justin Case.'

'Right, Mr Case. See you then. Nice to have spoken to you. Thank you for calling.'

'Thank you. I'll just drop you a note confirming. Look forward to the ninth at three o'clock. Bye.'

Very amicable. If only more calls were like that. But the point is this: we can usually steer any call in the right direction by figuring out how people's minds work.

Analyse: 'a short meeting, half an hour or so'. As well as being music to Jenkins' ears, this delivers a double message:

- You are implying: 'My time is valuable too, because I'm *successful*. And I'm *successful* because I'm *good*.'
- Your exit will be painless (for him). He won't have to use body language hints to get rid of you.

These two factors will help to promote a constructive meeting.

Analyse: 'Ideally, within the next two weeks'. Notice the flexibility of the meeting date. You are giving Mr Jenkins most of the control. 'Ideally' suggests no pressure, but it's a subtle indication of your preference.

If you follow a similar procedure to that outlined above, you will certainly have done everything possible to clinch that important first meeting. When the time comes, the meeting may well go on for longer than half an hour – not at your instigation, but at the other person's. Because they are so relaxed they end up asking all sorts of supplementary questions. And after they've agreed a contract with you they may apologize to you on the way out – for taking up too much of *your* time!

Telephone telepathy in action

We'll follow the fortunes of Anthony Bates as he attempts to arrange a business meeting, displaying – and not displaying – these **communication skills**. The scenarios could apply equally to *any* interaction of this nature and in *any* setting. The skills are **transferable** and are effective in promoting successful outcomes, *no matter who you are dealing with*. First, we'll look at how not to do it – the 'wrong' way – and then we'll look at the successful method – the 'right' way.

Situation 1

'Mr Clayton's office.'

'Hello. I'd like to talk to Mr Clayton.'

'Who's calling him?'

'It's Anthony Bates, from Top Notch Hotels.'

'May I ask what it's to do with?'

'It's something I'd like to discuss with him.'

'Has he spoken to you before, Mr Bates?'

'No, he hasn't.'

'Just a moment.'

'I've had a word with Mr Clayton. Could you tell me what it's all about?'

'Well, OK then. I wanted to come and see him about a new five-star property of ours.'

'One moment . . . '

'I've had another word with him. He's in a meeting, and he's rather tied up. He said if you'd like to write in, he'll get in touch if he's interested.'

'No, you don't understand. I'm only over for a few days. I have to speak to him. I can't put anything in the post.'

'I'm sorry but he's very busy.'

'So am I!' 🙁

Situation 2

'Could you give me the name of Mr Clayton's secretary, please?'?

'Yes – it's Karen Carpenter.'

'Would you put me through to her?'

'Putting you through.'

'Mr Clayton's office.'

'Yes, hello. Could I speak to Karen Carpenter, please?'

'Speaking.'

'Miss Carpenter – good morning. Can you help me? The name's Bates.' (Pause) 'My company is Top Notch Hotels. I'd like a quick word with Mr Clayton if he's available now.' ☺

'Well, I know he's rather tied up now. I'll see. Does he know what it's concerning?'

'He probably knows my company. Would you tell him it's about a new five-star property of ours that I think he'd want to hear about? If he's busy now perhaps you could ask him when I might have a few words with him.'

'Just a second, Mr Bates. Would you mind holding?'

'No – take your time, Miss Carpenter.'

'Mr Bates, he said he'll be free in around half an hour. If you leave your number he'll call you back.'

'No, that's OK. I'll call back in about 45 minutes.' ☺

'Very well.'

'Thank you. Bye for now.'

After 45 minutes:

'Mr Clayton's office.'

'Is Miss Carpenter there?'

'Speaking. Is that Mr Bates?'

'Yes. Hello again.'

'Putting you through now.' (Click)

'Richard Clayton speaking.'

Coffee break . . .

Many things in life b____ with a phone call, so the importance of telephone communication skills cannot be over-estimated.

Many people undergo a p_____ change when talking on the telephone. (How often have you found yourself asking: 'Is that the same person I was with yesterday?'?) They can become stilted, nervous, incomprehensible and brusque.

With the absence of facial expressions and other body language, choice of w____ and t____ of v____ become all important on the phone to provide feeling to any message.

Be aware of what's h_____ on the other end of the line – especially important in business calls. Whenever you are telephoning somebody, you are bound to be i_____ them doing something.

T_____ is all important on the telephone – calls may be terminated or shortened artificially because the person is busy or has company; this can mean the end of your p_____.

W_____ and w_____ n__ to speak are crucial decisions that have to be made by the caller, as they shape the eventual o_____ into either a positive or a negative one.

Chapter 8

'What the large print giveth
the small print taketh away.'

Anonymous

Negotiating for mutual benefit

Understand the psychology involved, to achieve the best possible result

- Logic or emotion?
- The psychology of a negotiation
- Negotiate on interests and needs
- Don't bring me problems, bring me solutions
- Other negotiating techniques
- Negotiating tips
- The environment
- Seating
- Negotiation overview
- Making concessions
- Game plan
- Concluding
- Negotiation in action

Three travellers in the 1950s were checking into a hotel in Las Vegas (they were in the 'Neon City' for the World Poker Tournament).

- They negotiated with the bellboy a rate of **$15** per room per night.
- They each handed over **$15** to the bellboy, making a total of **$45**.

- Later when the night receptionist arrived, he informed the bellboy that the hotel had been promoting a special 'poker rate' and that the rooms were only **$10** a night.

- So he kept **$30** for the rooms and told the bellboy to return the balance to the guests.

While going up in the elevator the bellboy figured that as the three guests didn't know how much the rooms should have been, they would be more than happy with *any* rebate at all. So he gave each of the three guests **$3**, making a total of **$9**, and kept **$6** for himself as a tip.

All well and good, but here's the problem. Each of the three guests finally paid **$12** for his room, a total of **$36**. The bellboy kept **$6**. That accounts for the **$42**. **What happened to the other $3?**

(Answer in the Coffee Break appendix at the end of the book.)

Every day of our lives, we spend a lot of time negotiating, even though we're quite unaware that we're doing so. Because much of it happens informally, we may not realize that any negotiation has taken place. Oh – and just because we do it every day, it doesn't follow that we do it proficiently.

We may think of negotiation as the preserve of trade unions and employers, or of CEOs during a takeover bid, or of the United Nations trying to bring together two countries at loggerheads, but it's much more than that. **In our interpersonal dealings, we are arch negotiators**. We negotiate over our pay increases; we jointly decide which DVD to rent, what restaurant to eat in, who'll mow the lawn; we sell houses, buy cars, negotiate compensation for a faulty freezer and play ping-pong with builders as they modify their price with each scratch of the head. The list goes on and on. You may have heard the maxim: *you don't get what you deserve in life; you get what you negotiate.*

Good negotiation skills are an asset because it's often the final stage in the journey of persuasion – **taking people along with you from point A to destination B**. All the other six skills that we've discussed will need to come into play, as empathetic listening, questioning, power of recall, attention-holding, choice of words and non-verbal behaviour become important constituents for reaching an agreement.

In both our business and private lives, we will often have **continuing** relationships with some of the people that we negotiate with, and so the ultimate aim is to reach agreement in a way that promotes **mutual** benefit. In other words, a situation where *both* parties win; a deal or situation that satisfies both sides and is done in a spirit of trust and honesty. It does not mean that:

- you have to sacrifice your own goals;
- you have to be concerned about the other party getting what they want.

That's for them to do. Your job is to satisfy your interests. The other party is responsible for doing the same for themselves. The ultimate aim can be summarized in one word: **agreement**.

Real life, of course, means that quite often the other party, be it your business associate, boss, neighbour, friend, relative, store manager or tradesperson, is not so well-versed in this 'two-winners' principle. The trick then becomes one of subtly turning the proceedings – using good empathetic questioning and listening skills – towards a situation in which each side derives benefits. So to recap, it's plain to see that there are two opposing elements in a negotiation:

- a *competitive* element, in as much as we want to maximize our own outcomes;
- a *cooperative* element, in that we have the desire to reach an agreement.

Two opposing goals. Small wonder then that no matter how much experience we've had, formal or informal, the task of negotiating is something that most people find difficult.

Logic or emotion?

As we discussed right at the outset on your 'path' to becoming more persuasive, most persuasion occurs *below* the level of consciousness. There are two paths that can be identified: **conscious** and **subconscious**. This applies to all of our interactions, be they in personal life or our working life. Human beings in and out of work show a lot of predictable behaviour. Being able to 'get inside the mind' of the other person is key to attaining a satisfactory outcome. Also, be aware of the 'type' of person (more of that in Chapter 10) you're in negotiation with. Broadly, think in terms of two types.

Is the type of person the more *direct* type who deals mainly in **logic** and **facts**? This person is:

- in a hurry to get 'to the bottom line' quickly;
- resistant to the 'gift-wrapping' of facts and ideas and makes an intellectual decision when they feel the proposition is right.

When you're stuck on a negotiating point, any deviance from their favoured direct approach to problem-solving of just cold facts and analysis can cause annoyance on their part – and you run the risk of a complete breakdown in proceedings, even though you'd managed to get so far.

So, when you've got beyond the first stage towards winning people over to your point of view and you're in that delicate second stage of negotiation, be aware from the behaviour and conversational style of the other person as to how to present your information.

After they've satisfied themselves with the logical side, **then the emotional side comes into play** from their subconscious (do they trust you/like you enough to make 'concessions' in order to progress?).

By contrast, the second type of person is more reliant on **intuition**, rather than cold, hard facts and information, and will *initially* make a decision on **emotional** grounds – how they feel about the situation and the person they're dealing with. As mentioned earlier, all research and real-life encounters show that for the vast majority it is the emotional side that reigns supreme. Having generated that 'feeling' they will then:

● look at the logic/information side to 'back-up' or justify their favourable decision;

● if they both 'mesh' they'll move to the next stage.

Neuroscientists have proved that the way our brains are wired means that **emotion reigns over intellect when it comes to the process of decision-making**.

In your personal life you probably have no trouble in analysing how you make decisions and it's probable that you readily accept that it's the emotional side that plays a big role in any decisions you make.

In your working life there is an assumption that all business decisions are made rationally – weighing up pros/cons, risks/opportunities, cost/benefit – and then a choice is made, but this is not the case. Emotions feature heavily in every decision made.

So, for both types in any negotiation process – low-level or high-level – there is always the logical and emotional side. Get inside the mind of your audience, identify the initial triggers and deal with the two types accordingly. You'll then find yourself 'negotiating without negotiating'.

The psychology of a negotiation

In the past, much theory and discussion were focused on ascertaining a **position** in a negotiation situation, arguing the case for it, gradually offering concessions and finally reaching a compromise. The essence of this is that your main objective is maximizing your own interests at the expense of the other person's. The annoyance of this type of negotiating is that as each person fails to achieve their 'position', there's a certain element of loss of face which results in one or both parties rigidly refusing to budge. It still goes on of course. You see it in everyday life all the time. An interesting example is a conversation I observed at an outdoor craft market while I was in New York, between a father and his son – on holiday from Britain – and the stall vendor who was selling crafts and second-hand books:

Son (to his father): 'Dad! That's a second-hand copy of the American first edition of *Harry Potter*.'

Father (to vendor): 'How much d'you want for that?'

Vendor: 'Yeah – it's a first edition. $250.'

Father: 'I don't think it's worth that much. It's not in pristine condition. It's a bit battered – and the cover's not good. I'm sure there are quite a few used copies around.'

Vendor: 'Sir – it's reflected in the price I'm asking. If you take a walk along 8th Avenue and go into . . . you'll see . . .'

Father: 'I'll give you $100.'

Vendor: 'That's being unrealistic, Sir. Like I said, if you walk along 8th Avenue . . .'

Father: 'OK. I'll give you $110. It's not in great condition. Take it or leave it.'

Vendor: 'I'll take $230. It's been a long day.'

Father: '$115. My last offer.'

Vendor: 'Can't help you, Sir.'

The father and son walked off. They were within my sight and were looking at other stalls. I saw them walk back towards the bookseller's stall (I just had to go back to watch!).

Father: 'OK. I'll give you $125 for that *Harry Potter*.'

Vendor: 'Look. I'll take $210. I've gotta pack up now.'

Father: 'OK then.' (His son snatched the tome from the stall before the dollars had even been exchanged.)

Well, it doesn't look as though the father was trained at Hogwarts School of Witchcraft and Wizardry; he wasn't able to use much magic on the bookseller. A 'muggle'? But then this was a classic case of **positional negotiating**. The father took a position, gave it up, then took another position, gave it up, and so on, and then finally he conceded. But he ended up paying more than twice what he originally offered. (He was definitely a 'muggle'!) The psychology of positional negotiation often goes something like this:

1 You make an offer that's perhaps a little extreme.

2 You then gradually make very small concessions just to keep the negotiating process alive.

3 The other side does the same.

4 An agreement is difficult, and the whole process becomes time-consuming and exhausting.

5 It becomes harder to alter your opening gambit as you keep trying to justify it to the other party.

6 A battle of wills occurs between the two sides.

7 As you constantly defend your position, you become more stubborn because it now becomes a question of your ego.

8 As you focus more on positions, your concern for the original interests (both your own and the other party's), which in our example concerned the purchase and the sale of a book, becomes *secondary*.

9 You're forced to base whatever course of action you pursue next on the previous positions you have taken.

10 Often this results in either no agreement or not the best one.

In the example above, the father (or rather the son) walked away with a Harry Potter book, but he altered his position considerably and was concerned not so much with ego in the end but with his own interests. Of course, in a situation like this, where the relationship is short-term, he was able to do this. **This was a classic case of win–lose, where you're concerned merely with getting as good a deal as you can**. But in a more formal business transaction with, perhaps, a long-term relationship, clearly this positional approach would be fraught with problems. If you stick on a certain position then you are insisting on a *specific* solution. In your eyes, this is the only thing that will work. It is very rare for there to be only one solution.

If we re-run the movie tapes, an alternative scenario in which perhaps the father states his interests whilst *acknowledging* the inevitable interests of the stallholder (which is to maximize revenue from his sale) – plus the provision of a face-saving reason for the vendor to justify acceptance of a lower price – might have gone something like this:

Father: 'Look, I understand what you're saying about a store on 8th Avenue. But this *Harry Potter* book is not in great condition; also take a look at these pages inside – these are torn, that's got marker pen smudges . . . '

Vendor: 'Well that's why I'm selling it and it's not in the used-book stores.'

Father: 'I appreciate that entirely. I'd be happy to pay you more – in fact I'd prefer to, because it would mean it was in better condition. But I showed you those pages.'

Vendor: 'OK. What are you prepared to pay? But only give me a realistic price, not the $115 you just mentioned. I know what it's worth and I know what I paid for it.'

Father: 'Well, in view of the general state of the book and those pages I just showed you, $150 to me is fair.'

Vendor: 'I understand your point about those pages. I hadn't looked closely at the inside of the book, I have to confess. In view

of that, if you'll accept what I consider is fair, let's call it $170. It's
been a long day – and I've got a broomstick to catch!'

Father: 'OK, it's a deal.'

In optimum scenarios, the position should merely represent a
starting point, and the objective is not to get stuck in the mire
of positions but to reach satisfactory agreement. This is easier
to achieve when we *substitute* needs and interests for positions in
any negotiating situation.

Negotiate on interests and needs

We've seen how positional negotiating, which may work well
in some simple situations, relies on the other party reciprocat-
ing with some sort of concession. This, of course, is not always
what happens, and therefore a stalemate situation can occur or
the parties may try to force each other into giving away more.

A far better alternative is to focus on the needs and interests
of each side in a negotiation. If we analyse what the **point** of
a person taking up a position is, it becomes obvious that it is
something that is designed to satisfy their interests.

Also, the individuals you are dealing with have various **needs** of their own. They are human and, therefore, emotional beings first and a client, boss, colleague, relative and so forth next. So, it is important that the working relationship is insulated from any disagreement about detail in any negotiation. Disagreement often leads to people getting offended or misunderstanding your point, and to fractured egos and the fabrication of blame. A sensitivity to the self-esteem needs of the people you are dealing with is essential.

When we are dealing in positional style negotiating, *the other party becomes part of the problem*, and so the situation becomes compounded. **So, it is essential that the people side of any negotiation or conflict resolution is taken out of the proceedings**. The last thing you want is for the people you are dealing with to become defensive. The focus should be on finding a solution to the problem. The problem is not the people you are dealing with. They should be treated with respect, with all due empathy displayed; above all, they should be listened to, regardless of whether you agree with their words.

When we delve *behind* positions, we can *identify* interests. After all, your interests are what made you decide to adopt a certain position. And, of course, if we start to think in terms of interests then it's easier to think of **shared** interests that two parties may have. It becomes more likely, then, that mutual agreement can take place, because it is easier to move together from common interests than from widely differing positions. (So, as Alice says in *Alice in Wonderland*, 'Everyone gets prizes.')

In addition, an important point is that usually there are many possible positions available for every interest. **Also, this approach eliminates the power and ego struggle that is a feature of the position approach**.

Before we move on, there's just a point that needs clarifying. Of course, if you sold your car, you would have liked more money for it. Of course you would have liked more for that old laptop of yours; that antique Victorian jug; your house that you finally managed to sell (after three offers fell through). **We mustn't get confused** when satisfying another person's interests and our interests with satisfying our *likes*. *You would have liked more money in each of the above instances.* But a deal was made that enabled agreement to take place with both parties because your respective interests were satisfied (at that time).

Don't bring me problems, bring me solutions

Miss X (magazine publishing director): 'So, can you tell me why that poses a problem? It's within the budget figure we discussed at the group meeting when your clients were present.'

Mr Y: 'Well, the idea of a hundredth-year celebration issue was fine. But I don't think we can go ahead with it now. I think we'll have to drop the idea because circumstances have changed for the client. An important piece for the issue will not now be available and so they don't feel it would be worth doing. I know we agreed in principle to go ahead with it at the last meeting. I appreciate the time you've put in.'

Miss X: 'Could I ask you what circumstances have changed?'

Mr Y: 'Well – in confidence Miss X, the clients are getting a new chairperson. The headhunters are shortlisting at the moment. They have a pretty good idea who it might be. But the idea was to have a chairperson's message in the issue. With your two-month copy deadline we wouldn't be ready. It was a good idea about the anniversary issue though.'

Miss X: 'When will the new person start?'

Mr Y: 'Probably about two weeks before the publication date that you had discussed.'

Miss X: 'Well, I've an idea. We could go ahead with the issue as planned. If you can get the chairperson's message to us shortly after they start, we'll produce it as a supplement and it can be incorporated in the issue.'

Mr Y: 'Are you sure you could get that done within one to two weeks?'

Miss X: 'Oh yes. As long as it's in the print schedule well before time. We'd book that in at the same time as the issue.'

Mr Y: 'What about cost differential?'

Miss X: 'Well – it's *their* anniversary. Tell the clients that for goodwill, we'll pick up the paper costs for the supplement run if they'll just pay for the machine time. Call it an anniversary present!'

Mr Y: 'That sounds great. Problem solved! I'll get the paperwork sorted out later today and then we can discuss editorial next week. You haven't got any other solutions up your sleeve have you? I've got a problem with this cat next door. You see, she keeps . . . '

In this example, the focusing on finding a solution, with no resistance but just a seeking of reassurance by Mr Y, has resulted in the glitch that threatened the survival of the project being *overcome* with some creative thought. By concentrating on the **underlying** interest of Mr Y, which was an anniversary publication that had to have the chairperson's message in it, Miss X came up with a solution and, by the look of it, generated some future goodwill. She gave away something that was *low* in cost to her and high in **perceived** benefit to the agency's client.

So, we can see that it's important in any negotiation first to work out what *your* interests are and then to delve into *their* interests. How do you do this? Well, as in the example above, it usually involves **asking**. When Miss X delved into the reason why it would now be difficult to go ahead, the other party revealed the exact reason. Of course, he did not know whether there could be a solution. Quite often you will get an idea of the other person's underlying interests through **empathetic listening and questioning** (something that, of course, by now you are already expert in). Questioning allowed Miss X to elicit valuable information from the client and it allowed her to display her empathy (which was good for the relationship) and, more importantly, resulted in a solution. I'm reminded of the irritating, but nonetheless important, mantra: '*Don't bring me* *problems; bring me solutions.*' In this fast-paced world of ours, both at work and in our personal life, isn't it what we all want?

Other negotiating techniques

As social animals we are all interdependent, but we will have interests that may differ from those of people we interact with. A great deal of the negotiation we are forced to engage in, therefore, derives from the following:

- Our interests are incompatible with another person's interests.
- Another person has interfered (or is intending to interfere) with our interests.

Result: conflict.

We've discussed the ideal win–win strategy, but not every encounter results in this quest for mutual interest and satisfaction.

Extensive research by social psychologists has shown that there are a number of different ways in which we respond to conflict, either in an everyday life situation or in a work and business setting. People will display a negotiation style based on one of the following five tendencies. **Which style is used depends on the circumstance and the 'players' that you are dealing with**.

1 *Competition*: the person tries to get the maximum possible for themselves and ignores the interests of the other party. You may use this style when you are:

   - encountering somebody who is perhaps aggressive and unreasonable;

   - sure of your ground and can prove that you are right (for example, when negotiating compensation from a store for a product that, as well as being faulty, has resulted in causing you loss of some sort).

2 *Accommodation*: give up and let the other party have all the benefits. You may use this style when you:

- want to let the other party have a favourable impression of you (or your organization) in order to foster goodwill for the future (typically, the concessions may be low in importance to you and *high* in benefit terms to them);

- have no chance of succeeding in furthering your own interests (and, therefore, to persist may jeopardize other areas);

- realize that you have made an error somewhere along the line.

3 *Compromise*: a cooperative approach – for example, to split everything down the middle. You may use this style when:

- you want to develop (or keep) a relationship;

- other 'styles' have failed to produce agreement;

- time constraints mean that a solution has to be found;

- you want to end the power struggle of two dominant players.

4 *Avoidance*: the desire to walk away from any kind of conflict. No effort is made to further your own interests or to seek to know the interests of the other party. You may decide to use this style when:

- there is little hope of influencing the situation in any way;

- the timing is wrong;

- feelings are running high and any further meetings would generate more heat than light;

- there are no benefits to be gained when weighed up against the human and economic costs.

5 *Collaboration*: a focus on maximizing gains for all parties (win–win). You may decide to use this style when:

- it is in the interests of the two parties concerned to find the 'two-winners' solution because of the nature of the transaction;

- a long-term relationship demands that both parties achieve mutual gains.

Essentially, research has shown that two scenarios are created: there is a situation in which the goal relates first to our wellbeing and second to the wellbeing of others. For example, accommodation is concerned more with others and less for ourselves; competition is more concerned with ourselves and less with others; compromise shows an equal preference.

What tactic is used is completely dependent upon the situation. But the most common method that we tend to adopt in problem-solving and negotiation is the one that maximizes *joint* benefit (the classic win–win).

Within **ongoing relationships**, we obviously negotiate in a different fashion to the way we behave with **strangers** and **acquaintances**. After all, within personal relationships, or among work colleagues, there is an unwritten law that we care about one another's interests.

Negotiating tips

The key to good negotiation – and therefore problem-solving – is to indicate clearly what you want. We all have a right to certain wants, needs and goals. Equally, there are situations where others have the right to block you if what you want goes against their best interests. But you must at least communicate your desires.

The next step is **listening** – really listening – to the other person's wants. As a result, the conflict is defined as a mutual problem that has to be solved.

Both parties, having stated what they want, must now express how they feel. This is something that most people find difficult. You may be angry, exasperated, shocked, afraid. But it's very important to share your feelings. You can show anger without being aggressive, for example. Anger and aggression are not the same thing. The other person then knows the effect that their actions are having on you.

Many conflicts are never resolved properly because **true feelings** were never disclosed. If anger is suppressed, because of a reluctance to disclose true feelings, and an agreement is made, then hostility may still remain and *future* dealings will suffer.

So, having expressed your feelings and the desire to solve the problem ('I'm confident we can work something out so that we're both satisfied'), you need to show that you can both achieve what you want. (Fact: for every need or want, there are usually several **options** to satisfy it.)

We often assume that because somebody takes a different line or position to our own in an interactive situation, then their goals are also opposed to ours. This isn't always the case. There are often shared and mutual goals as well as some that differ. Work out the differences between your wants and goals and the other person's. Where are they the same? Take a look at your common and opposing interests. It is often by sacrificing some of the opposing interests that you can build on common concerns and needs. You may then come up with a number of possible agreements to choose from to resolve the problem. The one that is fair to both and increases the likelihood of an amicable long-term relationship is ideal.

The environment

'**Where**' and '**when**' are just two important points that may often be overlooked when deciding on negotiation tactics. Will it be in the intimidating setting of your boss's office, the interviewer's conference room, the plush boardroom of GGA News Corporation, your lawyer's musty cubicle-size lair, the estate agent's busy open-plan office? You need all your senses about you; you want to ensure that listening to the other person will not be a problem (and, for him or her, that they can listen to you) and that the place is relatively free from *distractions*.

We've seen in Chapter 3 how difficult it is to control attention **when there is interference in and outside the head.**

If the other party does not concentrate then the chances of an optimum outcome are reduced. Visualize the **attention curve** from Chapter 3 and make the appropriate adjustments. Many agreements of a poor outcome (and no agreements) can be put down to **situational** causes such as a poor venue.

In a formal meeting situation, in which perhaps a number of people are present, the person or organization that is hosting the meeting on their premises will, more often than not, start the proceedings. This, of course, may give them some sort of control:

'I'd just like to confirm where we stand at the moment. We are unable to proceed along the lines that were outlined in your letter of . . .'

This means that you are immediately *responding* to perhaps some sticky points that you had intended to address later on in the meeting, after pointing out some favourable news that you've brought to the table.

Don't worry. It's still possible to seize the initiative and win back some control:

'Thank you for that recap of the situation as it stood a fortnight ago, but before we discuss that I'd just like to . . .'

If you have some sort of control as to who attends your meetings, exercise it. There may be people on the other party's side (and even your own) who actually *hinder* progress because of their personality type (see Chapter 10). Your aim is to negotiate a satisfactory agreement, and it's futile to have present someone whose cautiousness, demeanour or whatever may scupper any deal. Quite often, you'll hear people saying things like: 'What's your schedule like next week, Donna? We've got that guy coming in from TGC on Wednesday morning. I'd like your input.' Before you know it, you're suddenly negotiating with six people when your original meeting was with two people (six names to remember!).

It may be difficult to control the other side's exuberance, but be sure that *you* are not taking along people who don't add anything to the proceedings and who may actually prove a liability. And how may they prove to be a liability? In a number of ways: interrupting when the other person is speaking; putting doubts in the other party's mind; misinforming . . . The list is endless. On the other hand, you may take along an 'expert' who can answer technical questions, for example. But be sure that your 'expert' doesn't speak just for the sake of it; in other words, to justify being there. Many a negotiation has gone sour because of superfluous comments from a colleague who wanted to 'contribute', having been silent most of the time. In certain instances, less is more.

Seating

From a psychological angle, seating is so important. Ask any cat!

If you have the opportunity, **try to control the seating arrangements**. It's amazing how so many people take great care in choosing a table in a restaurant, and yet in a pressurized situation of a meeting they'll leave everything to *chance*, even if they have a choice.

So what does the psychological research tell us? Well, we know that the ideal table that promotes a non-confrontational atmosphere is a *round* one. It avoids the 'them' and 'us' of the long rectangular table, with the two sides sitting directly opposite each other. However, if you're stuck with this kind of table, then it softens the proceedings a little if you *don't sit directly opposite* the other party.

If there are a few of you, it often works out that you sit at each end of the table or even on adjacent sides, and this can take the **adversarial** nature out of the meeting. If you're going to the other party's offices then quite often you'll be taken to the room in *advance* of your hosts. That's the time to stake your claim as to the seating arrangements. When the others arrive, they will adopt the arrangement based on how you've spread yourselves out.

Equally, if you're waiting for your boss in their office, arrange your seat so that it's not so *formal*, in the sense of directly opposite, as it is when you go in there during your normal discussions with them. This is a negotiation about extra holidays and flexitime. You're looking for mutual interests. There's a shift in the balance of power (at least for a few minutes). If your boss's office has easy chairs or a sofa, so much the better.

Negotiation overview

Problem: **everybody wants to be the winner**. Who wants to be the loser? There's no fun in losing. But what constitutes a 'win' is normally subjective: it's in the mind – *your* mind.

The game of negotiating to win differs from all other games. That's because we're looking for two winners.

The process of negotiation starts only when something has been agreed upon in principle. You've made your case about your proposition or product or service; the other person is convinced and is in the right frame of mind to take it a stage further and accept – except for a few minor points.

What points? The obstacle could be trivial as far as you're concerned. But it's significant in the other person's mind. *And that's what's significant.*

It's a joy to watch professionals negotiating. Not just over products and services, but in the world of social affairs. Government ministers, for instance, negotiate every day; they trade concessions with other parties. It's exactly the same negotiating process, with both sides gaining something.

But many people do not understand the reasoning behind the principles of negotiation. They forget that negotiation takes place *after something has been agreed in principle*. You may persuade a potential employer that you are perfect for the job, but then fail to negotiate well on certain sticking points and so fail to get it. You may manage to reach agreement over the sale of your product or service, but then negotiate ineffectively and lose the deal. You can see, then, that the successful professional has to be master of the whole process.

The plain truth is that the majority of people are poor negotiators. An understanding of the psychology behind negotiation can really improve results. Let's define the scenario:

- You know that the other person wants a better deal.
- Equally, they know that you want a good deal.

Who budges?

No one can be blamed for asking for a better deal. ('I'd only consider taking this job if there were six weeks' paid holiday'; 'Well, if you'll throw in the security system and air-conditioning, I may pay the figure you quoted'; 'You'd have to include free after-sales service for all our sites if we're to agree to the costs outlined.')

There never was a truer maxim than: 'If you don't ask, you don't get.' But just because somebody asks for something, it doesn't mean it has to be given. If it's reasonable and settles things without too much aggravation, monetary sacrifice (if relevant) or bad feeling, fine. But if both parties are dissatisfied then the equation is not right. Remember – it's a game with two winners.

If one half of the negotiating equation is not happy, then the situation is also unsatisfactory. In any relationship, whether it be personal or workplace-related, if only one of the parties wins then the **relationship** loses. The aim is to satisfy the needs of both sides of the relationship to secure a win–win situation.

Consider these points in business:

- An unhappy client is unlikely to deal with you again, may pick faults with your product or service and possibly may withhold payment.

- Equally, an unhappy supplier of goods or services is unlikely to give good service during and after the transaction. The client wanted the concessions, but not at the expense of something else. That wasn't part of the scenario.

Making concessions

Since negotiation is essentially a trading of concessions, we're looking for an amicable compromise. Most commercial transactions today require some element of negotiation. Very few are simply, 'Yes, I'll take it.'

Fact: as consumers (and in the corporate world) we're not always concerned about better price, delivery or payment terms, and so on. **We don't like being sold to; we'd much prefer to buy (i.e. retain control).** Therefore, if we win concessions from the other person (on price, for instance), we feel that we have bought rather than been sold to (ego). In effect, there's been a reversal of roles; we've 'sold' to the provider of the product or service (so we, the customer, feel as though we've won; now, there's a switch!).

Have certain concessions up your sleeve that, if need be, you can bring into play. And perhaps have a major concession that you can be flexible about. But don't offer them all immediately; **leave something in the hat after the rabbit's been pulled out**.

Game plan

The other person's problem: 'I don't know what your bottom line is. I don't know how much you are willing to spend, or what you'll settle for ultimately. So I want you to make the first move.'

Your problem: 'I don't know how far I can push you on price, delivery or payment. So we'll play ping-pong until someone digs in their heels and refuses to budge. If that's me, you make the concession.'

You're treading a thin line all the time. If your original demand is too high, you turn off the other person and don't even get to the negotiation stage. And, yet, you've got to give yourself room to manoeuvre. If you give your bottom-line figure immediately, with no concessions (because you've already included your concessions in the 'package') then the other person won't feel they were ever in the match, let alone that they've won.

It's tough psychologically because you don't want to alienate the other person. After all, they're in the right frame of mind for accepting your proposition; it's just these concessions that they're seeking.

If you watch the pros negotiating (at wage tribunals, economic summits, in the boardroom, etc.), you'll notice how they let the body signal their response to a demand. You'll see them shaking their head, smiling, flicking an imaginary speck of fluff off their jacket, or giving occasional outbursts of laughter in disbelief. They're trying to let the other person know, without actually saying no, that the request is over the top. It's less offensive using body language.

The other person doesn't know whether what they've asked for is fair, and they're being given the signal that their reasoning is wrong. They may not seriously expect to get the concession – but they need to know how close they can get to it.

Getting inside the other person's mind is crucial here, as the other person's ego demands have to be met. **If you can work out the area in which their principal needs and fears lie, then it will help you to decide which bait you need to use** and how far you have to spread the net. They might be worried that a delivery let-down could lead to their own client raising a claim against them. In this case, you could offer to send the goods by overnight air freight at your expense. This would save eight days. They buy peace of mind from you: a *small* concession for you, but a *big* one for them. Deal done.

Generally, you'll be pushed (or only allow yourself to be pushed) up to the limit of the concessions that you're able to authorize. The other person can usually sense this from your own hesitancy and body signals. If they want more then you may have to consult with somebody. This can be both an advantage and a disadvantage.

The advantage is that you are out of deadlock and have breathing space to check and see whether there's anything else you can offer that can ease the situation. And, of course, you can actually consult with other relevant people to see whether you can go further (that's if you want to).

The disadvantage is that you've perhaps worked hard at building up momentum towards acceptance of your proposition during the face-to-face meeting and interest is running high (**remember the attention curve?**). Now you go away. This can change things. Say the person you are dealing with doesn't have a particularly good memory; they *forget* all the good points that they were so excited about at the first meeting. It's natural. So many things have happened since then: the roof fell in; they fell out with their boss; their company's lost a big contract; their health isn't good.

Their interest is not running so high. That's natural. You probably need to go through the whole process again. But they're too busy to see you now. They may even have seen somebody else offering something similar and agreed to this rival proposal on the spot. Timing is all important.

Concluding

If you want to avoid reaching stalemate and losing momentum by leaving to check certain facts, you should wind up the process. Produce the ace up your sleeve:

'OK, then. If we get the celebration concert CDs to you already packaged with your logo printed, and we do it within three weeks – at no extra charge – is that a deal?'

'You're on!'

You should emulate a lawyer summing up at the end of a court-room hearing at this final stage. The trick is to restate *what you're actually giving*.

During the negotiating process, people get so obsessed with the play in progress that they *forget what they've asked for*.

Analysis: by restating what you have just conceded to the other party, you are affirming psychologically what a good deal they have managed to get out of *you*. Game, set and match to *them!* (**Or is it to you both?**)

Negotiation in action

You might have seen the film *Sliding Doors*, in which two parallel situations occur based on whether the female character went back to her flat, or whether fate had caused the sliding doors to make her miss her stop on the train and not do so. Just like life. If you'd have done X this would have happened, but instead you did Y and that resulted in a totally different outcome.

Let's see how the story unfolds for our character, Anthony Bates, as he attends three meetings, and see if you can put *yourself* in the character's position in each situation. *See whether you (based on what you've read so far) understand the reasons for the* ☺ *'smiley' and 'not so smiley'* ☹ *faces.*

The first meeting

Situation 1

(To receptionist) 'Morning. I'm seeing Mr Burns at 11.45.'

'Your name, Sir?'

'Anthony Bates. Top Notch Hotels.'

'Would you take a seat?'

After some time, Mr Bates is led to an office:

'Good morning, Mr Burns.'

'Good morning, Mr . . . er, Mr . . . '

'Bates.'

'Yes. Sorry to keep you waiting out there.'

'That's OK.' (He sits down) 'It's a pleasure to meet you. It's good of you to see me, especially after the last fiasco at the conference you held at our Gstaad hotel. I hope your clients were not too annoyed. Must be a couple of years now. I heard about it at one of our regional meetings.' ☹

'Now, what "fiasco" was that, Mr Bates?'

'Oh – you know. We dealt with your predecessor, Mr Flint. The audiovisual company we'd arranged for you didn't turn up. Something to do with them losing paperwork that our offices had faxed to them. Some mix-up anyway.' ☹

'I see.' (Puzzled look. His mind is distracted now. He's intrigued to discover more about the previous dealings with this company that had let them down.)

'Now, Mr Burns. I wanted to talk to you about our new property in Cannes. It has excellent conference facilities, three gourmet restaurants and a top-of-the-range health spa.' (Reaches for his case and rummages around for several minutes. In the meantime, Mr Burns decides to make a call.) ☹

'Gary – hello, it's John Burns here. I have a gentleman from Top Notch Hotels here with me . . . Yes, that's right. Oh . . . sure, I understand. Yes. Oh, *did* they? Bye for now.'

'Here, I've got some floor plans and sample menus. This shows you the exterior of . . . '

(Burns glances at what is handed to him but is clearly detached from the proceedings.)

'What are the delegate rates mid-July, for around 200 or so?'

'Well, that would be high season, so let's see what we could do if . . .' (The calculator comes out and there is a long session of key-punching. Mr Burns's attention is drawn back to the pile of files on his desk, and anxiety starts to creep in as he surveys the debris.) 'Let me just give you this sheet here. I've scribbled down the reductions you would get if you switched from deluxe rooms to standard, and also there's some different meal plans there.' ☹

'Thank you, Mr Bates. Now, if you'll excuse me I've got some pressing work that I've just got to get finished. Thank you for coming to see me. I'll bear you in mind.'

'Oh, it's my pleasure. As I said, it's nice to make contact with your company again after the last unfortunate mess-up. Can I give you a call next week to see if we can arrange something?' ☹

'No, don't bother. I mean – I'll get in touch with you if I'm interested.'

'Bye for now.'

Mr Burns is left thinking: 'I'm certainly not dealing with them. They may let us down again. Good job he told me about it – I'd never have known. Before my time. That wouldn't go down well with the boss. Anyway, at those rates, who needs to take a chance with someone new? I'm still on my trial period here. What a waste of time that was!' As Anthony Bates gets into the taxi, he thinks to himself: 'That went well. I'm sure that won't turn out to be a waste of time!' ☹

Situation 2

'Good morning.' (Hands over a business card to the receptionist.) 'I'm seeing Mr Burns at 11.45.'

'Would you take a seat?' (Receptionist walks away with his card and returns shortly to accompany him to the office.)

'Good morning, Mr Burns.'

'Good morning, Mr Bates. Do sit down.' (Burns studies the business card.) 'I see you're based in Monte Carlo. Good weather there now. Better than ours, I suspect.'

'Just a little!'

'What have you got to tell me? Anything interesting?'

'Well, yes. Very, I hope. It's a new property we've acquired and completely refurbished in Cannes. Here's a brochure to give you an idea. You're still organizing overseas conferences for clients, I understand?'

'Oh yes, very much so. Matter of fact we're doing something this week over in California, in Palm Springs. To give you an idea of the kind of places we go for, it's an old favourite of mine – a period-style property. A top-rated one that also has a resort feel about it. It's in 45 acres with gardens, a lake, tennis courts and – do you play golf, Mr Bates? (Bates nods) Well, you'd like the 9-hole golf course. Good health club too, with an indoor pool. I do like their gourmet evening restaurant – they do great seafood dishes.'

'You're keen on seafood then?'

'It's because I'm always on a seafood diet. I see food and I eat it!'

'Ha! I know what you mean. My wife is always steering me towards it – keep the calories down!'

'I know how you feel. Down to business – we're using a lot of your competitors, as I'm sure you know. I've only been here two months now. I'm working on the programme for 2015–2016. So your timing's good.'

'I see.'

'I'll probably be interested in your other properties in other destinations, but tell me about this new five-star in Cannes. What's a typical rate based on 300–400 in September/October, which is something I've got to put together shortly?'

'Well, naturally it will vary according to the split of rooms you take. I've got a write-up on the hotel that was done last month. Perhaps you'd just like to have a quick look while I tot up some figures.' (Bates does some scribbling while Burns is reading the article.) ☺

'Very impressive, Mr Bates. Have you got a rough idea of the figures?'

'Yes. Here they are.' (Bates passes him a piece of paper.) ☺

'Does that figure include VAT, Mr Bates?'

'It doesn't – it's ex-VAT.'

'Makes the rates a little bit more than we're used to paying.'

'I understand. However, we would also include various day excursions for the delegates' partners to various attractions at no charge, every day.'

'I think we can work together on this one, Mr Bates.'

'What would you like me to do next, Mr Burns?' ☺

'I'll email you details on Friday. It's quite pressing on the schedule so I need to tie it up. It's been at the back of my mind for ages.'

'We'll be pleased to fix it all up for you.'

'Your timing's good, Mr Bates!'

The second meeting

Situation 1

'Ms Peters will be with you in a moment. Perhaps you'd like to go on into her office and wait, Mr Bates?' (Bates surveys the large office: an imposing circular table with three chairs; on the table, two half-full cups of coffee and a phone; numerous bookcases; at the far corner, a large mahogany desk covered in papers. He walks over to the desk, puts down his case and sits in the chair opposite it, removing a pair of gloves, which are lying on the chair. After a few minutes, since nobody arrives, Bates pulls out his laptop from his case and places it on the edge of the desk. ☹

Two minutes later:

'Ah, Mr Bates. Apologies. I just had to get these letters. My secretary's off sick today.' (Ms Peters casts a sideways glance towards the circular table by the door and then walks over to Bates, shakes his outstretched hand, notices the laptop that's perched on some of her important papers, pointedly walks to the edge of her desk and removes her documents from under the laptop.) ☹

'Oh, sorry.' (Bates closes the laptop and puts it away in his case.)

'Now, Mr Bates. It's about three weeks since you called me. Can you brief me again? You were interested in telling us how you could help us with the anniversary celebrations that we're planning. Is that roughly it? I'll just sign these letters while you're talking.' ☹

'Yes. We've got a brand new five-star property in Cannes and we have a ballroom that can accommodate up to 500 people. You mentioned on the phone that there would probably be 400–450 guests. Is that correct?' (Silence, as Peters is studying and signing her letters, her head down.)

'Sorry – er, is that correct?' (Pause) ☹

'Is what correct?'

'I was saying that you mentioned that 400–450 guests would be attending your anniversary.'

'Yes, about that.' (She gets up, walks over to an out-tray, puts in the letters and then returns to her desk.) 'Your rates are very expensive, aren't they, Mr Bates?'

(A knock on the door.) 'Excuse me, Ms Peters. Could you sign this petty-cash voucher for the milk? Mr Mollet is in Cambridge today.'

'Let's have a look at this, Sarah. What's this? £3.42, is it? I presume you've checked it's right, have you? Er . . . can somebody else not sign it?'

'There's nobody around, Ms Peters.'

'Oh, very well.' (Glancing at Bates.) 'Signing my life away again.' (Sarah leaves.) 'Now, where were we?'

'You were saying we were expensive.' ☹

'Yes. We can get a good venue in Marbella for less. What else have you got to offer?' (Bates takes out a large file and places it on the desk, covering a number of Ms Peters' papers. He takes out a loose-leaf floor-plan and passes it to her. Ms Peters is concerned at the file that is covering her pristine sheets of paper. She keeps checking out of the corner of her eye that they're not being mutilated. ('Should I ask him to move that heavy thing? No – I suppose I was blunt enough earlier.') This is a great distraction for her. Her concentration has gone. Then the telephone rings.) 'Yes. OK, Richard. I'll stay on the line while you look for it.' ☹ (Bates is staring directly at Peters and is showing, through the vernacular of the body, his impatience. Peters, sensing this, asks him to carry on talking and puts her hand over the mouthpiece.) ☹

'So you see, Ms Peters, even though . . .' (Peters waves at Bates to stop talking as she resumes her phone conversation.) 'Yes. That's fine, Richard. We'll pick up on that later. Bye.' (She shows signs of being preoccupied again as she loses eye contact.) 'Look, Mr Bates, leave that brochure of yours. I'll look through it when my secretary comes back. I'll ask her to put down our requirements and write to you. Now, have we got an address? Did you give me a card?'

'No, sorry. It slipped my mind. Here.' ☹

'Oh. You're based in Monte Carlo. Tell me – that restaurant by the casino. Haven't been there for years. Guy with a patch over his eye used to run it. Is it still there? Can't for the life of me remember the name. I used to go there regularly when I worked in Nice. Wish you'd have mentioned you were based there earlier. Liked to have had a chat. Anyway, must dash now – let me see you out.'

Situation 2

(Bates walks into the office. The large desk by the window is covered in papers. The circular table looks a better bet. Peters obviously uses this area, as there are two half-empty cups left there. He sits down at the table. From his case he removes some papers.) ☺

'Mr Bates – apologies. I just had to get these letters off today. My secretary's sick.' (They shake hands and Ms Peters sits down at the table.)

'Mr Bates, it's three weeks since you telephoned me to arrange this meeting. Now, remind me about your proposition to do with our anniversary bash that we're planning. If you don't mind I'll just run through these letters for mistakes and then I can sign them. You carry on talking.'

'No, that's OK. You carry on with your letters while I get some paperwork together that I'd like to show you.' (Bates finishes shuffling papers when he sees Peters return to the table after having deposited her letters in a tray.) 'Right.' (Bates hands over his business card; Ms Peters reciprocates.) ☺

'Mmm . . . ' (Peters is studying Bates's card.) 'You're based in Monte Carlo. I worked in Nice for a while, many years ago. I didn't know your group was owned by BMM.'

'Oh, yes. They bought us last year.'

'Do you know a chap called Scott Walker?'

'Yes. He's running North America now. He's president. Well, not *the* president!'

'No, quite. I worked with him about 15 years ago in Rome. If you're talking to him, say hello from me.'

'Sure I will. Now, our new hotel in Cannes has a ballroom that caters for up to 500 guests or delegates.'

'What rate are we talking about here, roughly?'

'Well, we can base it on the type of room . . . '

(There's a knock on the door.) 'Excuse me, Ms Peters. Could you sign this petty-cash voucher for the milk bill? Mr Mollet is in Cambridge today.'

'Let's have a look at this, Sarah. What's this? £3.42, is it? I presume you've checked it's right? Have you a pen? Look . . . er . . . are you sure there's nobody else to sign it?'

'Nobody else is here, Ms Peters.'

'Oh, very well.' (Turns her gaze to Bates.) 'Signing my life away again . . . Now where were we?' (Bates picks up on the fact that Ms Peters is the type that doesn't like signing things in a rush – and that was just £3.42 for milk!) ☺

'I'll just recap. I was saying that we can go up to 500 people in the new ballroom and your costs can come down substantially if you take a different spec of room to the deluxe. ☺ Here, let me show you a picture of the brand new standard rooms. They've got all the facilities.' (He stops *talking* while Peters studies the literature.) ☺

'These rates are a little bit higher than the proposal we got in for the hotel in Marbella. Would you be able to include transport from the airport within these rates?' (Bates nods to show agreement. Then there is a telephone interruption.)

'Sorry about that. What was I saying?'

'You were saying that you'd like us to include transport within the cost, which we'll be happy to do. I can guarantee that will be OK.' ☺

'So what would that be for 460 guests roughly? It's that column here on the matrix: is that right?'

'Yes. Do you want to take things a stage further?'

'Yes. I think, subject to a few nitty-gritty details, which I'm sure we can sort out, we may be able to celebrate our important anniversary at your new hotel.' ☺

'Yes, and if we make sure it's successful, which we'll aim to do, you can come back again 200 years later!'

'Well, you're a little younger than I am. I don't think I'll be able to make it!'

'I'll put some details to you in the post, urgently. And I won't forget to say hello to Scott for you.'

'And remind him he owes me five million lire – or whatever that is in euros now. Plus interest! Bye, Mr Bates.'

The third meeting

Situation 1

'Do come in, Mr Bates.'

'Thank you, Mr . . . er . . . er . . . Hitchcock.'

'By the way, Mr Bates, I'm sorry about last week. I know it was short notice, but it was unavoidable. These things happen, as you know.'

'What happened exactly?' 🙁

'You remember – I mentioned to you when I telephoned to cancel our meeting. I had a burst pipe at home; the whole house was flooded. I seem to recall you saying you had this problem last winter.'

'Did I mention that to you, Mr Hitchcock? Oh, yes . . . That's right.' 🙁

'Anyway, you've got some interesting overseas hotels, you said on the phone.' (There is a knock on the door.) 'Oh, Holly. Come in – sit down.'

'Thanks.'

'I'd like you to meet Mr Bates of Top Notch Hotels . . . Mr Bates, this is Holly Wood, our locations manager.'

'How do you do.' (They shake hands.)

'Mr Bates felt that their new five-star in Cannes and some of their other hotels around the world would be of interest to us in the coming year. Do you want to tell us a little more?'

'Sure.' (Bates shows them various photographs.) 'You'd be well taken care of with our DBC programme, so I'm sure you'll find there'll be no problem as other film clients that have been on DBC have been very pleased with the arrangement. In fact, DBC offers more than . . . ' 🙁

(Hitchcock is distracted; he's wondering what on earth DBC can be. He's nodding away but isn't really listening. He doesn't want to ask and appear ignorant – especially as Miss Wood doesn't appear to be showing any non-verbal signs that she might be having trouble with the jargon. He is now preoccupied with playing word games in his head in an effort to guess the answer. Mr Bates should have said what it is, he thinks. ('It's obviously significant. Still, never mind. I've missed most of what he's been saying now. I don't know how he expects me to be interested if he doesn't spell out essential details . . . Now, where am I supposed to meet Eileen for lunch today?') Bates tries to reclaim Hitchcock's interest as he sees they've lost eye contact. But he can't grab his attention by using his name, because he's forgotten it. ☹ Now the telephone rings.)

'Hitchcock speaking.' (A blessing for Bates as he now knows his name, again.) 'Yes, come up, Beverley. I'm in the middle of a meeting but you may find it interesting.' (Shortly afterwards, there is a knock on the door.) 'Come in, Beverley. Can I introduce you to Beverley Hills, Mr Bates. This is Mr Bates of Top Cat . . . sorry, Top Notch Hotels. He's come over to talk to us about some new properties. Grab a seat.'

(Bates promptly offers some of the paperwork to the new arrival. He then looks over to Hitchcock.) 'What did you think of the comments relating to our superiority over similar venues in the area, Mr Hitchcock?'

'Well, it seemed to be very . . . ' (He hadn't paid attention.)

'One-sided?' ☹

'Well, I suppose you might say that. I feel that the hotel is more suited to . . . '

'Film companies with bigger budgets?' ☹

'Well, maybe.'

'Yes, I thought you might say that. But with out-of-season rates tumbling, you'll find that they're very competitive for a hotel of this calibre.'

'Is it possible to have a . . . ?'

'Think about it?' ☹

'Well, I was going to say, is it possible to have a look at that photograph again? But now that you mention it, perhaps we can put our heads together and we'll get back to you at some stage.'

'If you need any more information, please call me.'

'Yes. We know where you are.'

'Well, I hope you get your roof sorted out, Mr Hitchcock.' ☹

'Er . . . I beg your pardon?'

'Your roof – hope it all works out.'

'Yes. Quite.'

When Bates leaves, the three colleagues discuss his shortcomings:

'That fellow is worrying. Didn't ask any questions.'

'Didn't look you in the eye, either. He had no empathy for our particular needs. Was only interested in prattling on, even when I was trying to read his PR blurb.'

'Now, listen, Holly, you know about location hotels and all that. It's driving me crazy. What the deuce is DBC?'

'Pass!'

'Beverley? Come on – you must know!'

'Funny you should mention that. I've been dying to ask you two!'

Situation 2

'Do come in, Mr Bates.'

'Thank you, Mr Hitchcock.' (Sits down as directed.) 'Well, what happened with your burst pipe in the end? Was there much damage to your house?' ☺

'Oh, that! Don't ask! The place is in an absolute mess. We can only use one room. My wife's still distraught. The insurance company have been in; they've given the go-ahead to get the repairs done immediately. I've just got to find some decent builders.'

'Oh, I am sorry. I sympathize with you, having had the same problem last winter, as I mentioned to you briefly on the phone.' ☺

'Yes. Did you get your repairs done satisfactorily? Any problems?'

'No, it was relatively smooth. We found a very competent firm of builders. They're used to dealing with flood damage – they work really fast. As a matter of fact, I think I've still got their number in my organizer here. If you're interested you could perhaps get an estimate.'

'That would be a great help. I'd really appreciate that.' ☺

'Here it is. Noah's Construction Ltd. I'll just jot down their number for you.'

'Thank you. Now, we'd better get down to what's brought you here, or you'll be missing your plane! We make films and television commercials, as you know, and in the original letter that you sent to me, you mentioned a particular hotel of yours that might be suitable for some of our work.'

'Yes, I've seen the kind of work that you do. You tend to go for period-style properties, don't you?'

'Well, we like to find the ideal location. We're doing something in Switzerland at the moment. Our crew are staying at one of the large 5-star, modern hotels we use in Geneva. You would know it – the Mövenpick Hotel. Easy for our production people to get around as well. Handy, being close to the airport and they have a shuttle bus.

The cast and the directors are staying in what was originally a castle. Privately owned, of course. All the rooms have authentic period details dating back to when it was built and you couldn't wish for more comfort. It's a real time-warp experience. And their restaurant is a treat.'

'A lot of hotels dish up mediocre food.'

'Yes, quite.'

'A lot of our places have superb settings. Just have a quick glance at this. This is our new property in Cannes – it's already got a reputation for its cuisine.' ☺

'Oh, Sandra . . . Coffee, Mr Bates? Right. Sandra, would you mind? Two coffees . . . '

'We get a lot of film crews staying at many of our hotels throughout the world. We're fortunate, I suppose, that they're mainly in superb settings. And they're predominantly older historic properties.'

'That's very interesting, Mr Bates. We've got a few things coming up – you've made me think. Oh, by the way, I've asked our locations manager to come and join us. She's got a few problems at the moment so she's in a bit of a tizz. You know how people let you down all the time. Let me try her line in case she's forgotten.' (As he picks up the telephone, there's a knock on the door.) 'Come in. Ah, Holly, there you are. I was just ringing you. This is Anthony Bates of Top Notch Hotels. I mentioned him to you.'

'Hi. I'm Holly Wood. Nice to meet you.' (They shake hands.)

'Good to meet you. Sorry, I didn't quite catch your name – Holly . . . ?' ☺

'Wood. Holly Wood.'

'Right. Thank you.'

(They all sit down and Bates hands his business card to the new arrival.) ☺

'Holly, Mr Bates was showing me particular hotels that might be good for some of our shoots. Perhaps you'd like to continue, Mr Bates. What were we saying?'

'You were telling me that you've got a few things coming up shortly that we might be able to help you with.' ☺

'Yes, that's right.'

(Bates hands a brochure and some photographs to each of them. When they have both finished reading and Bates can resume *eye contact*, he continues talking.) ☺ 'As you can see, as I mentioned to you earlier, Mr Hitchcock, they're historical properties and are popular with people in your line of work. During the low season, some film companies will take over the entire hotel, and cast members and crew are resident there for long periods.'

'Yes. I wouldn't mind a long spell in those surroundings – eh, Holly?'

'And of course, when you're with us in any of the hotels, you're designated DBC clients. Since we've been running the DBC programme it's been a huge success. In fact, DBC has resulted in us receiving an award last year, it was held in Hong Kong, and . . . ' (He notices by their body language signals that they're losing the thread.) 'Oh, forgive me, I'm going on about DBC all the time, assuming it means something to you. It's our "Doing the Best We Can" programme, which is a sort of VIP programme for preferred clients. We offer a whole lot of extras and guarantees of service and the scheme won us an award last year.' ☺

'That's very good.'

'In fact there are a few paragraphs about it in this press cutting here, if you'd like to take a look, Miss Wood?' (He looks over to Mr Hitchcock while Miss Wood is reading.) ☺ 'When you're shooting commercials, is there an average length of stay that you're away?'

'Well, as Holly will tell you, it can be anything from four days to a month.'

(Bates looks towards Hitchcock's colleague, who is engrossed in reading the press cutting that he handed her. She has seen something interesting on the same page: a recipe for 'the world's best sticky toffee pudding'.)

'Is that right, Miss Wood?' ☺

'Sorry, I'm getting carried away here, Mr Bates. I was just reading something else on this page. Very interesting.'

'Our hotels, or the sticky toffee pudding?'

'Both!'

'Mr Hitchcock was just telling me that when you're on location shooting commercials, the length of time varies a lot.' ☺

'Yes, it sure does.'

(The telephone rings. Hitchcock answers it.) 'Yes, come up, Beverley. I'm in the middle of a meeting. You might like to meet the gentleman.'

(A few moments later, there's a knock on the door.) 'Come in, Beverley. This is Mr Bates. He's from Top Notch Hotels. Beverley's our budgeting director on the film side, by the way.'

'Hello – I'm Beverley Hills.'

'Pleased to meet you, Ms Hills.'

'Let me see. Top Notch Hotels. Didn't I read something about you in *Film News* recently? Some award or something like that? Or maybe it was some other organization.'

'That was us. Excellent memory, Ms Hills.'

'I remember it because it showed a picture of one of your hotels with the crew of *ESP – The Nightmare Begins* standing outside the front. A friend of mine is in that film.'

'I was showing Miss Wood a recent write-up of ours.'

'D'you mind if I take a look?'

(Bates then addresses Miss Wood.) 'What do you think of the facilities that we offer on DBC?' ☺

'It seems to be very . . . comprehensive. Seems to cover all angles.'

(Bates now directs his gaze at all three.) 'I should mention to you that we've got a rate that includes all meals and, if it's not possible to take them on the property – naturally I appreciate that some of the crew are out a lot – then a suitable packed meal is provided.' ☺

'What rate are we talking about as an average, Mr Bates?'

(Bates passes a sheet of paper to each of them. After studying the figures, Ms Hills turns to Bates.) 'Mmm . . . a little more than what we're typically paying with the contract rates that we've been getting from certain properties, but then . . . Mmm . . . I suppose we're talking about something that's a bit different, maybe?'

'Yes, indeed. Do you mind if I ask, Ms Hills, what happens with the crew as far as meals go in other places you've used?'

'Well, they tend to eat in the hotel and, if the hotel doesn't have the capacity, they'll go out somewhere. Naturally, it's all on expenses.'

'Does that sometimes lead to you going over budget on certain productions?' ☺

'Sometimes? I wish that were so. More likely all the time!'

'So, you've got no control on their spending when they eat in the hotels, if they can, and also when they're out? I suppose there's all those taxis as well?'

'That's true.'

'So, if you paid a slightly higher rate with us, which includes meals, then it probably works out the same as the figure you're used to – or probably even less, I imagine.' ☺

'Yes, less I would say, looking at the restaurant bills I have to sign off!'

'So, you'd get better cost control and also your crew would get guaranteed seating in the hotel for their meals and wouldn't have the inconvenience of having to go out.' ☺

'Sounds good – keep them under control!'

Twenty minutes later, after Bates had left, Mr Hitchcock, Holly Wood and Beverley Hills discuss the meeting:

'That was very interesting.'

'Yes. I think we can use them a lot. They've got some great properties in just our kinds of locations.'

'And those rates aren't bad at all, really. With the meals thrown in, our bottom-line figures could look a lot healthier.'

'Yeah, and the clients might then give us some leeway with those other things we've been suggesting to them. Could be good. I liked that chap . . . Blake – no, what am I talking about Holly – was it Blake? Age, you know – creeps up.'

'No, Mr Hitchcock. You'll have to use a memory technique like mine – "association", the "experts" call it – I just think of the Bates Motel!' ☺

Coffee break . . .

§ In a classic win–win negotiation situation, the two competing elements of c_____ and c_____ are always present.

§ Just because another person's p_____ is opposed to yours, it does not mean that goals are opposed.

§ To negotiate in good faith, you need to build a reputation for t_____ and h_____.

§ Win–lose negotiations are usually concerned with relationships that are t_____ in nature.

§ Don't negotiate on positions. Negotiate on i_____ and n_____.

§ Where long-term relationships are concerned, the w___– w___ scenario is the usual one.

§ Good l_____ skills are probably the most important asset for negotiating.

§ The key to good negotiation is to i_____ clearly what you want.

§ Remember – negotiating takes place only a_____ something has been agreed in principle.

§ Negotiating is essentially a trading of c_____ that results in amicable compromise. The win–win is subjective.

Chapter

9

'Life's not fair. If life was fair, Elvis would still be alive and all the impersonators would be dead.'

Johnny Carson

'Difficult' people (and their behaviour)

Who are they?

- Expectations
- Boundaries
- The procrastinator
- The explosive
- The rigid
- The self-important
- The untrustworthy
- The antagonist
- The dampener
- The extrovert

Let's take a look at a species that comes in the form of work colleagues, bosses, subordinates, clients, customers, friends, relatives and so on – all bound by that one tag: the 'difficult' person. (In Chapter 10 we'll examine the various psychological 'types' that walk the planet. You'll be able to categorize these people based on scientific research.)

Survey after survey continually show that as far as the working world is concerned, the number-one reason for people changing their jobs (followed by seeking higher pay and promotion) is to escape from difficult people. Research into employee engagement in recent years reveals that many people cite a poor relationship with their boss as a reason for leaving.

Typically, they'll go to another job and find another difficult boss and more difficult people; and the process continues.

Frustrating. 'It's not fair,' they'll bemoan. But that's how it is: life's not fair.

There are two areas that contribute to altercations with 'difficult' people: first, in the area of **expectations**; and second, in the question of **boundaries**.

Expectations

Let's look at expectations. Psychoanalysts are constantly trying to realign their patients' expectations. Whenever you have an expectation of something or someone, **there is a good chance of big-time disappointment**. Result: friction. So people (and you) become difficult.

It could be the flowers you expected from your husband or boyfriend (you'd have thought *one* of them would remember!). At work, let's say you're expecting your PR person to get you blanket coverage in the press for the company's latest results; another manager is expecting his senior sales person to somehow magically come up with contracts that will more than pay for the huge cost of the exhibition stand; a team member expects her manager to remember that she's worked late six times this quarter and that she deserves a pay review.

The tragic thing about many of the instances just described is that quite often these 'expectations' *have never ever been voiced*, let alone discussed with the other person!

These expectations are *entirely in the person's head*. Small wonder that when we then react in a certain way towards people we feel have let us down, we can become labelled as difficult. And on the other side of the coin, they become 'difficult' in our eyes because of their original sin, plus how they've reacted to hearing about our disgruntledness.

As a consequence, you'll find in the workplace the whole hierarchy of the company, from top to bottom, walking around and harbouring resentments against different individuals over **unfulfilled** expectations: team member with other member of team; subordinate with manager; manager with his or her boss.

How do we deal with expectations?

The only way to **break the cycle** of unrealistic and unfulfilled expectations is to tackle the problem with the person at source. If you think you have friction with someone because of expectations that you have set for them, or alternatively you have a grievance against someone because of the expectations they have set for you, it is only by discussing it with the person responsible that the situation can be resolved. If it's a workplace grievance, the tendency is to down another pint or a glass or two of Sancerre with colleagues after work and vent your anger to them, or discuss it with friends or relatives. *So the problem of difficult people quite often never gets resolved* and we move on (with relationships and jobs). The point is that most people become less difficult after a discussion out in the open.

Boundaries

The other area that contributes to friction, as discussed earlier, is the notion of boundaries. Psychologists always talk of physical boundaries and emotional boundaries. In the soap-opera world of work, with the amount of 'masking' that inevitably takes place, we assume a number of roles, and so the concept of boundaries is alive and real. A PA can be difficult by, for example, working at your desk while you're away, interrupting you in private meetings or taking phone calls that are meant for you. A member of the management team might say yes to something that's your decision, in your absence, because he thinks it's a good idea for the company as a whole. Equally, a boss can be difficult by not observing the boundaries that are implicit within your role. This undermines your relationship and will often destabilize your interactions with your staff. Dale Carnegie put it well: *'Dealing with people is probably the biggest problem you face, especially if you are in business. Yes and that is also true if you are a housewife, architect or engineer.'*

Change your approach

We have to be clear from the outset about one thing. It's all about how we manage these people and the situations. They're not going to change. **We have to change**. Before you say, 'Hey, just a minute, I'm not the problem ...', we're dealing with people with their own *realities*. They think they're right and you're wrong.

You can't just walk away from friends, relatives, lovers, work colleagues. So, develop the skills and self-confidence to **change your approach**. It's not a question of changing your personality. Just show some empathy and get 'inside the mind' of the 'difficult' person and learn how to take control – *rather than them controlling you.*

The secret: establish the type of person you're dealing with and try a new form of communication with them by changing your approach.

Lucy at a drinks party receives the unwelcome attention of the 'creep' at the other corner of the room – a payroll clerk:

'Oh no, he's coming towards me ...' (she groans to her friend).

'Hi – I'm Simon. Couldn't help noticing – great hair. Don't tell me – you're a top stylist in a swanky salon to the stars.'

'No. I'm a dental hygienist.'

'Oh, right. Err ... great teeth by the way.'

'What do you do?'

(Using his imagination and a 'puffed out' chest.) 'I'm an airline pilot.'

'Oh really? Airline pilot. Well, I've seen your approach – now I'd like to see your departure!'

So, again the solution is to tackle the situation at source with the transgressors. There are too many difficult people (many of them oblivious to their status) lurking around both in and outside of work.

Let's be realistic. If we're after better outcomes, the responsibility always falls to us when it comes to handling the different people that cross our paths in our personal and professional lives. We're all 'difficult' at times – none of us can be exonerated from this. There are, however, certain categories that exhibit a mode of behaviour that can be irritating or cause conflict from time to time. Let's take a look at examples of the most common ones you're likely to encounter and suggest how you can persuade them to tone down their difficult behaviour. (You've probably been all of these people at one time or another!)

Procrastinator

Explosive

Rigid

Self-important

Untrustworthy

Antagonist

Dampener

Extrovert

The procrastinator

We've all come across these people. It may be an internal member of staff or a potential prospect or client that just can't make decisions. We even engage in this behaviour ourselves when we're trying to decide which pizza to choose. **Making decisions is tough on all of us, both at home and at work**.

Quite often the procrastinator won't make a decision because there are many *different* variables to consider which makes the prospect of actually making a decision too daunting. This can be very frustrating if, for example, you've been talking to the facilities manager about a new state-of-the-art copier and graphics machine and she's been putting it off, like she does with every other potential purchase because she doesn't like making **decisions**. Or a client who sits on brochures and statistics after a presentation and is quite happy with that (for the long-term!). Quite often these people just don't like the idea of making a **mistake** and they need a number of other options in order to feel that they've researched carefully. **So give them more information**. These people are constantly looking at the potential downside of a decision. Procrastinators are prone to the '**Yes, but**' style of conversations. 'Yes, but I need to make sure of .... before I can decide whether ...' Know this type of person? A relative, friend, somebody at work? They like facts and figures and are always looking for *proof*. Proof that something is so. Their natural scepticism makes them doubt the validity of most things. This type doesn't even believe that the refrigerator light goes off when you close the door – *where's the proof*?

The important thing is not to show through your conversation and body language that you are irritated with them. You'll need empathy to get to the root of their indecision and also sympathy for their predicament (having to make a decision). Then you can set about helping them through a process that will unfold at their pace.

The explosive

Some people exhibit an explosive burst of anger that happens almost instantly (think Incredible Hulk) and renders them out of control. You may have seen it at an airline check-in desk – if you're lucky enough not to have had a boss or work colleague put on a show for you. The characteristics of this person's behaviour are that after this short onslaught they are usually ashamed at their **loss of self-control**. Because of this, a reciprocal loss of control by you, and the venting of anger at the person for blowing up, usually makes things worse. The explosive is already experiencing a degree of self-loathing for his or her actions.

The anger may have been directed at us, for something that we did or didn't do, or something that we said. Equally, sometimes it may be directed at a situation, or the world. So – what does experience tell us to do? Well, we need to try to curtail their tirade. A placatory 'keep calm', or words to that effect, usually makes things worse. A statement about how angry you are at witnessing them being angry doesn't usually help matters either. **It's their show and therefore it's their agenda**.

You need to get their attention by using their name at a volume that can be heard above their rantings. Then show concern and listen for the reason for their outburst and show empathy. Keep good eye contact so that the person feels you are listening. Although it's tough, show that you understand why the person may have had the thoughts that led to the outburst (that's not the same as agreeing) and then work on moving to the next stage.

These people can be very intimidating. It could be a boss or partner who's quick to show offence and be angered and therefore retains his or her power base and control through exhibiting this behaviour. The key is not to show vulnerability and a diminution of your own self-esteem. You're dealing with a brain that's urging you to either fight or take flight. Is it any wonder that in this situation we may say or do things that seemed perfectly OK at the time, but we later regret? So don't play into their hands. Keep calm, maintain good eye contact and concentrate on the 'psycholinguistics'. Try words that will diffuse this show of anger, demonstrate cooperation, whilst at the same time maintaining your original stance:

'I appreciate you could have a point there ...'

'We're not getting very far with this today. I'll go back and take a look again and let's see if we might be able ...'

The rigid

It's difficult to get these people to consider any other possibilities that are put to them because their approach is rigid and the most frightening words in their lexicon are 'contradiction' and 'change' – especially *any change from what they have decreed is right*. They like **detail** and **minutiae**, and any invitation to change results in an analysis of what's wrong with the 'proposal' rather than what is right. They'll ignore any kind of 'big picture' analysis because they don't see life that way. They may be more introspective than other people and therefore have a tendency to be slow in responding to requests anyway. This makes them very difficult to deal with if you have to report back to somebody else.

They are so set in their ideas, which they regard as irrefutable, and they'll wield statistics to bolster their argument. **They prefer to use numbers to make their point rather than the power of prose**; it's easier to confuse people that way. But more often than not these figures and statistics have been 'tortured' to force them to make a point. Tortured? An economics professor of mine used to coin an imaginative phrase during his rants against politicians: '*If you torture figures enough, you can make them mean all things to all people.*'

They are so rigid in their knowledge that they're right that they'll be contemptuous of people's questions that challenge their way of thinking: they take it as a personal affront. So much so that you may not have the courtesy of a response to your questions, despite an assurance that *your* points will be dealt with, after they have made *their* point. Eventually, you may just run out of time. So no dialogue: one-way traffic. An absolutely cracking example of this, from the world of politics, was witnessed in the House of Commons:

The clunking fist clunked. Gordon Brown raged like an injured but still lethal pugilist. The injury was mainly to Mr Brown's feelings: George Osborne had just accused him of making an atrocious blunder with our pensions.

But Mr Brown's feelings are extraordinarily sensitive. The idea that he is not infallible is to him the most intolerable heresy . . . So Mr Brown rose in his wrath and declared:

'*I relish this debate. I will answer every question put to me.*'

It is Mr Brown's misfortune to live in an era when our leaders must pretend to delight in the cut and thrust of debate. This man, who hates being interrupted or contradicted, had to promise to take interventions from Opposition MPs.

But for a long time Mr Brown did not allow anyone to get a word in. He brushed aside the Tories competing to challenge him with the lordly rejoinder: '*I will give way to all of them once I have set out my argument.*'

A little later, Mr Brown said, '*I'll let people in once I've finished*', followed by '*I'll give way*', then '*I'm just about to give way*', followed by '*I'll give way now*', after which he at long last gave way.

The Chancellor then declined to answer almost every question put to him.

All politicians want to set the terms of debate but it is dispiriting to witness the sheer thoroughness with which Mr Brown rubbishes or ignores all arguments that are unhelpful to his cause. Julie Kirkbride (C. Bromsgrove) asked him why, if he was so confident of his own case, he had tried to prevent the application under the Freedom of Information Act for the documents showing the advice he was given by Treasury officials about the pensions decision. Mr Brown began his reply: '*First of all, we introduced the Freedom of Information Act.*'

This produced laughter for the Chancellor was making the preposterous suggestion that he is in favour of freedom of information. Yet Mr Osborne, leading for the Conservatives,

had already sketched in an amusing, but damning, way how the pensions plan was hatched in secrecy by a tiny cabal of Mr Brown's cronies while Labour was still in opposition.

Daily Telegraph, 18 April, 2007

When you're dealing with a difficult person like this (as you'll see in the next chapter), you don't get very far with empathy. All you can do is talk their language, which is detached and facts-and-figures oriented. Try to get into a dialogue by mirroring their obsession with facts and figures, and phrase your proposition in an analytical way.

The self-important

We come across these people in the workplace and in everyday life. Generally they are concerned only about themselves. They don't even think they have to put themselves in another person's shoes. Consequently, they see the world only from their own perspective.

You know this type – a condescending tone and body language that screams superiority. Ignore their arrogance (quite often it's a mask) and resolve not to let it get to you. Understand that they are looking for utterances from you that convey weakness that they can seize upon – so choose your words carefully and be sure of your facts.

Resist the temptation to embarrass them in front of other people. This rarely goes down well and may result in you being the 'hunted'. Revenge is sweet for this type of person. Since it's all about a change of approach – we can't change people – feel free to bolster their ego, if it helps your cause:

'I'd be happy for you, with your wide experience, to suggest a brand you consider trustworthy for ...'

'They sound like perfectly realistic points that we ought to consider ... could you help me ...'

These people are so preoccupied in showing the audience how important they are that there's no room to assimilate what you are actually saying to them, or the viewpoint that you're trying to convey. Sometimes it's a reverse psychology. That boss of yours is trying to cover up their feelings of inadequacy, so adopting this self-important tone or image provides a protective shield. The important point, as in much personal interaction with other people, is not to take things personally. They're playing a 'role' (an irritating one at that), so – as with your dealings with any kind of difficult person – **separate the behaviour from the person**.

These people like validation of their self-importance, so a simple acknowledgement of this at the beginning of your request (in the interests of moving forward) often works wonders. ('I can see that your mind is on that high-powered VIP conference that's going on in the hotel today – that must have taken some organizing, I bet – but can you get the concierge to find out for me if . . .'; 'I know you're handling these multi-million pound villas in Chelsea at the moment, because the launch date is near, but I'd like to view that one-bedroom flat that's advertised . . .')

These people like to be asked questions about their work or activity – after you've passed the first hurdle. It appeals to their ego and encourages them to 'thaw' a little.

The untrustworthy

When you consider the importance of trust in forming good relationships and in the process of persuasion, it's evident that dealing with untrustworthy people makes life just that bit more difficult.

As we've seen earlier on, trust is something that is conferred on you by another person or others. It's a feeling people have about you. Any time you deal with somebody and they've let you down, perhaps more than once, then, as Jack Welch says, you 'consult your gut' and decide how you feel about the person.

We come across people who just lie and people who are prone to exaggerate. Much of this in everyday life goes unchallenged and unnoticed and the world keeps turning. We're all guilty of it occasionally. But if a person develops a reputation for being unreliable, prone to exaggeration and telling lies, then that can be detrimental in our everyday life. In the workplace, which is all about interpersonal relationships, it's often very damaging, whether it's a colleague, your boss or a subordinate who is causing problems. Sometimes it's their insecurities that make them behave this way. Sometimes they think that by outwitting someone it makes them super smart. It gives some people a power kick.

If you want to tackle somebody about their untrustworthiness then the rule about focusing on their behaviour applies, so as to avoid defensiveness. We know from psycholinguistics (see Chapter 6) how damaging the 'you' word can be, so forget about the personally wounding Wild West bar-room talk: 'You're a no-good liar' or 'I don't believe a word you say, dude.' If we concentrate on the behavioural then it leaves the door open.

'Is there a reason why these final figures don't tally with the figures given to us at the time of our signing the contract?'

'We were told at the outset that there were no other offers on the house, which is why we arranged a survey. We need an explanation.'

'I was given the impression that there was absolutely no chance of the despatch date being altered by more than one day.'

Probably more than any other action, **untrustworthiness affects all of us in our personal lives and in our place of work**. Handled delicately, you can tackle the difficult person and point out the error of their ways. But in many cases it's a lost cause.

The antagonist

A very difficult person to deal with. There's a continuum for antagonistic behaviour that moves from ignoring, to unfriendliness, to rudeness, sarcastic remarks and bickering. Sometimes you know what's causing it. At other times you have to try to guess. There are some people who are antagonistic or aggressive because they feel that is the only way to get results. At work, for example, it becomes a self-fulfilling prophecy whereby behaving antagonistically towards staff and colleagues results in them behaving aggressively in return. A spiral of unpleasant aggression is created, and so the department, team or company as a whole becomes a hostile environment. People find that dealing with this kind of behaviour from another individual at work leaves them emotionally drained. (You may have seen examples of this kind of behaviour in the popular BBC series *The Apprentice*.)

What we may call **high-level** antagonism is usually directed at you personally. So you need to get to the bottom of the person's problem. **Lower-level** activity can be sarcasm, blaming, dismissing you or your statements, not listening to you and/or hogging a conversation.

Sometimes these people are unaware of the effect they have on other people with their style of delivery. It can become completely ingrained in them as a mode of communicating, **and if they're already low on the 'emotional intelligence' quotient**, unless they are told about it, **they just carry on upsetting people**.

Asking questions to unearth the problem in a sensitive way is the best way forward. Open-ended questions should be used:

Kate: 'There seems to have been a problem between you and me ever since I moved to this department. Can you give me an inkling of what I'm supposed to have done? And if I have – how can I undo it?'

Richard: 'Well, it's not you exactly. It's just that Andy [their boss] had said that I would get to handle the BWM account. But when you joined you got it as part of the package of clients that Sarah handled before she left.'

So, it looks as though something could have been done about this before. Perhaps their boss forgot what he'd said. Perhaps, also, Richard should have reminded him, instead of sulking and taking it out on Kate.

So, take responsibility and get to the bottom of why things are happening. The delicate way that Kate dealt with the antagonist helped open up a dialogue.

This type of person responds to a tentative style of language from another person. Their natural resistance to things means that if information is presented in this manner it reduces defensiveness on their part – and they may actually *listen*. So, for example, you may say to this person:

'It may have escaped your attention, since you've been very busy, but ...'

'In my opinion ...' as opposed to 'It's obvious to everybody that your ...'

When you're interacting with this type over contentious or difficult topics, the forceful approach (paradoxically) renders you *less* persuasive; speaking in a tentative fashion commands more attention with less resistance.

The dampener

You know this kind of person. You'd love to ask them the question:

'Do you light up a room when you walk in?
Or is it when you walk out?'

They put the dampeners on everything. You dread talking to them. That sinking feeling when you see them or when you hear them on the other end of the telephone. They come with a package of annoying habits and traits.

If you're in a meeting with them they stifle any kind of creativity you had. Even your personal life is at risk:

'Ken and I are going to Paris on the Eurostar on Friday.'
'No, you shouldn't go to Paris at this time of year. There's a nice caravan park in West Wittering – good rates at this time of year.'

'We're thinking of organizing a fun run for the local care home in April.'
'No, it rains in April.'

Many of these people lack self-awareness and are oblivious to their doom and gloom nature. If you're in a meeting with them they're probably talking to their shoes or their pencil. You don't see much eye contact. Their mind can't afford to be distracted by looking at you as it needs to work out plausible counter statements for anything that's suggested. They tend to be good on detail, and as they counter your proposal or suggestion they'll typically bore you with a mass of superfluous facts and figures.

It's important to remember that this difficult person's behaviour is not designed to be awkward. **It's just how this person is**. They're a particular personality type, for better or for worse. They may jump from idea to idea as they put the dampeners on your suggestions, and so you often need to curtail a conversation with this person as they pile on more and more reasons for you to digest (even after their refusal).

The extrovert

A short and final word on this less appealing of the extrovert species. Beware those who give extroverts a bad name and go beyond Carl Jung's definition (see Chapter 10). They are highly irritating due to an extreme hunger for attention. You'll encounter them in the workplace, where their craving for constant attention leaves no room for your feelings and requests.

They tend to lack empathy as they spend their time trying to be noticed. If you have a boss like this, then you will need to be self-sufficient because they probably don't have much time for you. Being the centre of attention is just that. There's no time for you.

If they're part of a team they can be high maintenance – and usually don't last. Overcome the temptation to prick this person's balloon if you want to get on with them. They want adulation and compliments. You can let them have this and then add your own comments and opinions after you've acknowledged their 'worth'.

These people are essentially '**narcissists**'. So they'll spend their time indulging in narcissistic behaviour. Their motto is: *'That's enough about you. Let's talk about m-e-e-e-e!'* So, when they've finished talking about 'me' and you bring the conversation back to you and your needs, bring the extrovert back down to earth. When they promise to do something or agree to that request of yours, ask them to put that in writing, or drop you an email to confirm. They may resist, talking about 'trust' and all that, but stick to your guns. At the time – especially if you've assuaged the narcissist's thirst for flattery – they'll promise a lot. And they may forget a lot, too.

Because they're so busy performing most of the time, they are particularly bad at picking up **non-verbal behaviour**. So your body language and 'paralanguage' does not register, which results in them not picking up your concerns and displeasure. As you know, we all have subtle methods of using bodytalk so that we don't have to voice our negative reactions. **We prefer people to pick up these micro-expressions and other non-verbal cues**. It's a tacit agreement in our interactions with other people. But the only way to get through to the extrovert is to stop them and point out your concerns. Otherwise there's more frustration because these people have to be stopped in their tracks as they 'railroad' through their ideas. 'Yes, Roger, I understand that it will benefit the whole department. But I feel that if we take that route, there won't be a *department* to benefit.'

Be careful when criticizing this person as the same 'highs' that dominate their behaviour can also produce extreme 'lows'. Although they may lack empathy and sensitivity towards other people, they can be sensitive to their *own* feelings (or ego, as Freud would attest). A reminder again: **focus on their behaviour** and leave the 'person' out of the equation. It's easier to take criticism about a behaviour (which is a one-off action) rather than us as a person (more personal and has a degree of permanence about it).

You can sometimes use this type of person's natural urge to show off to great advantage. If you have something difficult to do, or something that the extrovert has asked you to do (if it's work, we may be talking about a boss or superior), get them to do it! Of course the request needs to be 'gift-wrapped' first. 'You know Sophie. I've tried my best but when it comes down to it I think there's only one person who stands a chance of pulling this off. Can you give it a go?'

Of course when they've pulled off the deal, or whatever task you chose to relinquish, it's time for praise again. We know that this is what motivates the extrovert. Recognition is all. To shore up acquiescence for future tasks, give your praise in a visible fashion. Tell people about it and let the extrovert know that other people know about it. If you get the chance, praise this person in front of other people. Mission accomplished!

In the next chapter we'll take a look at the various personality 'types' that have been identified and draw upon the psychologist Carl Jung's classifications. We'll also look at how best to deal with each type.

Coffee break . . .

- The two areas that result in altercations between people usually have their origins in either e_____ and/or b_____.

- The Procrastinator is always looking at the d_____ of any decision, so give them more i_____.

- Generally when dealing with the Explosive it helps to show that you u_____ why they may have had thoughts that led to the tirade (it doesn't mean you're a_____).

- When dealing with the Rigid it may help to mirror their l_____ and thought processes by phrasing your proposition in an a_____ way.

- The Self-Important needs v_____ of their status in order for you to proceed to the next hurdle.

- The Untrustworthy is prone to e_____ and l____ so when tackling them about certain issues, concentrate on their b_____ to avoid defensiveness.

- Antagonists are often low on the e_____ i_____ quotient so use o_____ ended questions to unearth reasons for their attitude.

- The Dampener is often not deliberately a_____, it's just their particular personality style.

- Because the Extrovert exhibits n_____ behaviour you can often achieve your objective with this person by p_____ them in front of other people.

Chapter

10

'Clarification does not *explain* the individual psyche. Nevertheless an understanding of psychological types opens the way to a better understanding of human psychology in general.'

Carl Jung

The personality spectrum
How to identify successfully and deal with different 'types'

- Identifying and dealing with various 'types'
- Sensing and intuition
- Thinking and feeling
- Tips on influencing the various types
- Types you might meet
- How do you come over?

We have looked at the **seven** essential skills that are necessary to win the hearts and minds of those we are dealing with:

- good listening skills;
- how to hold attention;
- appreciation of body language;
- memory skills;
- knowledge of the impact of words (psycholinguistics);
- skills with the telephone;
- negotiating skills.

We'll now take a look at people's personalities. We've been doing it all our lives anyway. Haven't we? Sometimes not very complimentarily too, I bet. It's far better for us to make it a positive and enjoyable pastime. With a wealth of research from applied psychology, we now know a lot about *identifying* and *dealing* with our fellow human travellers.

Knowing or being able to work out the 'type' preferences of the people you interact with helps you in your quest to get them to side with you and go along with your ideas. As a clue to determining their preferences, you'll simply:

- observe their behaviour;
- listen to their language.

This will help you to decide what strategy to use when trying to persuade them to pursue a particular course of action. Personality defines a person's **attitudes**, **perceptions** and **beliefs**, and so a recognition of a person's 'type' can help in all instances of interpersonal communication in our day-to-day life. So, whether it's for work relationships, home life or any other situations, knowing or guessing a person's type preferences can be invaluable.

Psychological research into the study of personality types has centred on the aspect of **personality traits**. Psychological typing categorizes a number of related personality traits. There is almost universal agreement that we are a product of both nature (biology) and nurture (experience).

Psychologist Carl Jung maintained (in contrast to his colleague Sigmund Freud) that humans are not merely shaped by past events but also progress beyond their past. A keen observer of human behaviour, Jung noticed the diversity *between* personalities and also the consistency *within* a given personality. He could see by the way in which different people approached new situations that there were definite 'types' within the population.

Identifying and dealing with various 'types'

Some people are cautious and circumspect, while others are daring and adventurous.

Knowing and classifying a particular 'type' gives us an idea of the different ways people have of interacting with other people. It shows us their preferences.

Introversion and extroversion

Jung's major contribution was the concept of **introversion–extroversion**. The introvert and extrovert preferences are relatively easy to spot, *but the meaning is commonly misunderstood.*

Jung maintained that every personality directs its psychic energy towards what he called 'introversion–extroversion'. It describes how people are *energized* in life. An attitude of introversion turns a person towards their inner or subjective world of *thoughts, concepts* and *ideas*, where the source of energy is within and comes from solitary experiences. Such people don't necessarily need external sources for fulfilment; they prefer concentration rather than interaction, which they often find debilitating. **Reflection is more important than action, and they tend to plan and think carefully before doing things**. The attitude of extroversion, by contrast, is an outgoing one in which the external world is all important and *people* and *material things* are significant.

According to Jung, even though these attitudes are opposite, each person possesses *both*, and one attitude is dominant over the other. The dominant one is expressed in conscious behaviour, while the subordinate one is representative of the person's unconscious.

As we go about our everyday lives, we meet people who are open and friendly; the label 'extroversion' would probably apply to them. This does not mean that they are any more emotional or caring than those with an introversion perspective, who may be more reserved in a social setting. The latter may be quite adept at dealing with people but less relaxed with strangers; they may need to know people well and may prefer smaller numbers.

You may have encountered a situation such as this on an aeroplane. You've read the safety instructions, done the 'clunk-click' of the seatbelt, and now it's time for the in-flight magazine. The lady by the window to your right strikes up a conversation.

'I've been staying with friends in Edinburgh. What about you?'

'Oh, it was a company meeting with the usual boring speeches', you reply.

'Did you have to speak?'

'Oh no. It was just the people from our international offices.'

That's the end of your contribution!

How much do you now know about her?

> She hates flying . . . her husband's away on an oil rig . . . he got her a cat for Christmas . . . she's got dampness in her dining room . . . she refuses to eat anything that was once alive . . . her friend Doreen has bought a new hat . . . oh, and her son Mark has got a verruca (true, you embarrassed yourself by asking 'What year is it?' because you thought it was a car – instead of a foot complaint – but at least you got to say something!).

She obviously knew nothing about body language, as she failed to pick up the signals; not that there's much body available when you're strapped tightly in an economy-class seat, but the facial expressions and yawns should have done the trick. All you managed to convey to her was your poor knowledge of cars and that this was your first trip to Edinburgh. At first sight, we might confidently put this lady in the category of extroversion.

You could have plugged yourself into your iPod for half an hour and, after removing it from your ears, found that you were still being talked at. It's not that you didn't want to seem rude, you weren't *able* to be rude; you couldn't get a word in edgeways. Then the shaking of your hand at the baggage reclaim carousel where she announced with a moist eye that you were 'the best conversationalist I've met for years'. You'd barely been allowed to say more than 25 words! What's that old chestnut about the best communicators being the best listeners? (Remember Chapter 2?)

Since behaviour is *relative*, it's as well to remember that somebody with an extroversion tendency can appear to another extrovert as though they are an introvert, as that person may have a stronger extroversion preference, and so the two different extroverts will display quite different behaviour.

Extroverts tend to respond quickly to situations and often speak without thinking properly. In meetings at work, for example, or perhaps at seminars, the extrovert type of person will make themselves noticed, whereas introverts are usually more cautious by nature and think more about what they are going to say. It doesn't mean that they talk any less, as observing those with an introversion preference in a one-to-one situation may show.

There are advantages in being an E (extrovert) or an I (introvert). The E person may get more out of life in terms of happiness and satisfaction due to greater interaction with other people and a better support system. The I person is less reliant on other people for self-fulfilment, and their image is often one of being attentive and sincere (even if that's not the case).

If they don't understand each other's differences, an E can be perceived by an I as shallow, and an I may seem withdrawn to an E. As far as disadvantages go, the E can be a bit overbearing sometimes and come across as superficial, while the I may be criticized for having poor conversation skills and an apparent lack of interest in certain situations.

Jung's observation was that we all use both types. For example, a person is quite capable of being outgoing at work but more self-absorbed away from that setting. You've probably come across people socially or in the workplace who aren't that comfortable in the pub or wine bar at lunchtime with a large group (and for whom the 'best' parties are the ones that are cancelled!), but who are completely different one-to-one or in a very small group.

Characteristics of extroverts

- They tend to speak rapidly.
- They tend to speak loudly.
- Their energy level often *increases*, and they become more enthused as a conversation develops (like our lady on the plane).
- They tend to be quite animated during a conversation and use a lot of non-verbal (body language) communication – hand gestures, facial expressions, etc.
- They quite often interrupt a lot.
- They tend to speak a lot – and their sentences are often long.
- They tend to repeat their points and to overstate.

Characteristics of introverts

- They tend to speak slowly.
- They tend to speak quietly.
- Their energy level often *decreases* as a conversation develops.
- They don't use much non-verbal communication (e.g. hands and facial), and they may appear aloof and reserved.

Our success in influencing others usually involves 'matching' the other person in the early stages, in order to gain rapport, and so a knowledge of whether you are dealing with an E or an I and their associated style of operating (as listed above) is invaluable. **If you operate as more of an E and you are trying to get your point across to an I, then more often than not you will have to adapt your style more to theirs during your interactions** (as they would have to do for *you*).

The other important contribution of Jung was his analysis of the four functions that relate to how we come to know the world and understand it. By combining this with our knowledge of the broad picture of a person's E or I style, we can attempt to ascertain the best way of dealing with an individual.

Sensing and intuition

Jung's first dimension described how we are *energized* (either introversion or extroversion, as described above). His second dimension relates to what he terms **senser** (S) and **intuiter** (N).

This describes what a particular individual pays *attention* to in the course of their daily lives – their preferred way of taking in information.

For the S, the focus is on *facts and the use of the five senses*. The person who engages in sensing is taking in the objective world through perceptual processes, through the senses. When finding out information or making decisions, they tend to be practical, observant and skilful in remembering facts and processing them, i.e. a methodical person who pays attention to detail and is good at tasks involving repetition.

This person's workplace environment is often a mess, covered with files, papers, magazines, etc. and the desk is usually piled high and chaotic (don't say to this person: 'Could you put your hands on that cutting I gave you yesterday?').

The N pays attention to the vision of *what could be* and also engages in the use of the sixth sense. They relate to experience that cannot be articulated and rely on imagination, constantly on the lookout for fresh ideas and stimulating projects. This type likes variety and new and different experiences, and they may work on many different jobs all at once.

This person's working environment is usually crammed with a number of bookcases housing reference books, statistics and other abstract information. The desk is usually full of current projects and various books.

Thinking and feeling

This third dimension relates to a person's preferred style of making *decisions* – whether we use thought or personal values – and the two categories of **thinker** (T) and **feeler** (F).

The T person relies on intellectual processes – *reason and logic*. Any decision will be based on the logical results of actions, and they will decide impersonally. This type finds emotions to be a hindrance to the decision-making process and may be quite oblivious to the *feelings* of other people. Their approach is one of detachment (outside the 'self').

This person's working environment is usually orderly and tidy, with a desk that is, apart from a few papers, often very bare, save for the pen-and-pencil holder, stapler and container of paper clips.

For the F person, the keyword is *emotion*, and logic may not play a significant part. This person uses an evaluative process whereby things may be judged as either pleasing or painful. Decisions will be based on their personal values, on what matters or is important to them or to other people. They may be motivated not to cause distress or hurt to other people as they commonly show a lot of *empathy* (as opposed to the T person: if they do show any concern, it would merely be sympathy). They will often let the heart rule the head (unlike the T).

The F person's working environment is usually quite 'homely' and may have pictures, framed certificates and a group photo of the last awards dinner adorning the walls. The desk may have family photos and the odd gift from a member of staff, along with a golfing trophy or other award.

So, to recap:

- We take in information and make decisions as two separate functions.

- We take in information through *sensation* or *intuition* (not by both).

- The S person prefers to deal with facts, verifiable data and attention to detail.

- The N person prefers to look for possibilities rather than deal with facts, and prefers to look at abstract concepts and solve new problems.

- Having taken in information, the next process is one of making judgements, and we do this by either *thinking* or *feeling*.

- The T person is inclined to use logic and reason as opposed to personal values, and they may be oblivious to any emotional considerations.

- The F person makes decisions based on their own feelings and will take a course of action after considering its impact on other people.

A person's decision-making style, based on Jung's findings, derives from the four psychological states. One of these is the dominant function (i.e. S, N, T or F), and it is usually paired with one of the two from the opposite function, so that it is a combination of the two preferences. The four types have been categorized as:

Sensing – Thinking (ST)
Sensing – Feeling (SF)
Intuitive – Feeling (NF)
Intuitive – Thinking (NT)

Tips on influencing the various types

The first consideration is to identify the type of person you are dealing with, and then to adapt your approach so that it addresses the way the person thinks (mind-reading again). In our dealings in everyday life, we no doubt find that the people we are drawn to (both in and outside work) are people we can relate to because **their dominant personality style is similar to our own**. What about the other people? We usually adapt our interaction with them based on the traits that they exhibit.

Let's take a look at the styles and ways of achieving successful outcomes with these types.

The ST person focuses on **specifics and verifiable facts, likes stability and certainty, makes practical decisions in an impersonal way,** focuses on the present, likes to deal with realistic goals and deals with things in a logical way. So, when dealing with this type of person:

- Emphasize what can be achieved in the short-term (i.e. immediately).
- Prepare well and have facts and any other data readily available.
- Explain things in a logical fashion.
- Conduct your dealings in a business-like and detached manner (as he or she will), leaving the 'personal' side out of the proceedings.
- Avoid talking too much (long sentences and waffle).
- If the interaction ultimately relates to money being spent or invested, emphasize value and savings.

The SF person focuses on **verifiable facts, believes in personal loyalty, trust, being helpful and friendly,** and values these qualities in people they are dealing with. They make decisions based on realism and by weighing values and considering others. So, when dealing with this type of person:

- Use all your natural empathy to conduct things on a personal basis after you've got to know them better.
- Look for shared interests.
- Back up your attentive listening with positive body language.
- Highlight the benefits to them of your proposal.
- Conduct the discussion in a methodical step-by-step manner.
- Convey your friendliness by going out of your way to do or provide something for them (they operate in this way, so it's appreciated).

The NF person recognizes a wide range of possible opportunities and decides by weighing values and considering others. This type is **enthusiastic, values personal relationships, teamwork and cooperation, and has a love for new ideas**. They like to have a positive impact on other people and value sincerity. So, when dealing with this type of person:

- Ask lots of questions and then listen a lot.
- Show your natural friendliness during your interactions.
- Try to 'go with the flow' of what they want, and adapt as necessary.
- Don't inundate this person with detail; get the acceptance first and leave practicalities to the end.
- Highlight what is new in what you are proposing.
- Check the body language (especially paralanguage) for any disagreement or confusion (perhaps you were using jargon); this type often never voices their concern, so you have to look for 'leakage'. Then question to unearth any concerns.

The NT person prefers a variety of possible solutions, and then selects by impersonal analysis. They like to **analyse and create logical options, look at the big picture and focus on the long-term, and like to be thought of as resourceful and ingenious**. So, when dealing with this type of person:

- Probe for their own ideas at the outset.
- Show that you recognize their vision/concepts, and beware of giving the impression of being patronizing.
- Concentrate on business (or whatever you're discussing) quickly and save any 'personal' conversation (if at all) until that's been addressed.
- Accept that this type may bombard you with critical comments (they tend to spend time testing you so as to judge your competence).
- Allow them freedom to manoeuvre if this is possible (they like options).
- Focus on the long-term to make them feel comfortable.
- Be logical in your proposals, and emphasize cause and effect.
- Be punctual and well organized.

Although we have the capacity to engage in *all* of these functions or traits, as with introversion–extroversion we tend to rely on *one* of them. They help to define our personality. When we are trying to influence a person whom we mentally classify as being of the same type as us, it should alert us to the elements that we may be overlooking. For example, if two STs are in discussion, they may discount the effect that their proposal might have on people in general because of their 'blinkered' views.

You will meet people all the time who have to make decisions after hearing your point of view. **Many misunderstandings occur because of the *differences* in personality types, and so**

an insight into a person's style of operating and thinking can reap enormous dividends.

Types you might meet

We're all a blend of different types, but when it comes to clients, employers, etc. there are some real **stereotypes** that you will come across in your daily professional life. Identifying them allows you to adopt the appropriate techniques for handling them. With your knowledge of psychological 'types' from the previous section, have some fun and see if you can place them in the appropriate category.

You've almost certainly met some or all of the following types.

'Get on with it – give me the bottom line'

Not too difficult to fix up a meeting

This type is willing to give most people a chance if he or she approves of their initial approach. Somebody who didn't waste too much of their time on the telephone, for instance, would probably be granted a meeting (you may have telephoned this person about a possible job vacancy, or you may want to discuss your product or service).

They like to keep up with what's going on. If it's a possible 'superstar' job applicant or somebody that is offering a new product, then they don't want to miss out to the competition; they don't want to be left behind. This makes them want to know more.

Talks quickly

This is symptomatic of the rest of the personality. *Time* is constantly on their mind. In fact, they probably look at their watch at regular intervals while talking to you. They don't make any attempt to do this surreptitiously; they're blatant about it. *Their* time is being spent; *yours* doesn't enter into the equation.

For this type of person, time is money. 'I can't spend too much time . . . ' is one of their frequent sayings. Their secretary judges the status of visitors by how much time the boss spends with them. Time is the measure of success.

Coffee comes within three minutes

It's been ordered well in advance and brought in by a secretary with an endless smile. They probably have their own mug with some sort of inscription on it (ego-boosting), bought for them by someone in the office as a present – and a dig!

If you finish your coffee in the first five to ten minutes, it's easier to get thrown out; so take your time. If they turn out to be only half-interested, or they've lost the gist of the conversation because of interruptions, they may well grant you only as much time as it takes to drink your coffee. It gives them an indication of the earliest point at which they can terminate the meeting. You need time to bring them back on the right track. *It wasn't your fault there were interruptions.* So take it slowly and keep the coffee cup within their line of vision.

You can unnerve this type if they think that you have temporary control over the proceedings. If you want to stay (and you've finished your beverage) then sip *imaginary* mouthfuls from your cup (like they do in the soaps).

Studies you intently

This type maintains steely eye contact with you (when not looking at their watch) while you're speaking. They're listening only for *key* words that might be of interest. The rest of the time they're checking you out: clothes and body language – speech, mannerisms, signs of nervousness.

Desk shows a lot of activity

Because this type likes to be in on the action, their desk is covered with a lot of visual 'noise' (that's why they'll sometimes

meet you in the boardroom or another meeting room). Small wonder they don't like wasting time. If they sat around seeing people like you all the time, they wouldn't be visible from your side of the desk.

Wants you to get to the point quickly

This is the essential hallmark of this type. They like people who cut through the flannel and are succinct and sincere. They're worldly-wise enough to know what is what, so they want your message to be *straight*. If they sense waffle and double-speak then they start to show signs of impatience (their body language is easy to read, as they don't try to suppress it).

If that's allowed to happen, you're sunk. This type of person is thinking of a thousand things at once; if you ramble on, they'll just switch on to some of the other 999 things.

Essentially, this type can be a blessing to deal with if your pitch is right, whether you're selling yourself for a job, or selling a product or service, or whether you're trying to persuade them of a particular viewpoint. They will always want to buy you first; and if that hurdle is overcome, they will deal with you on their terms. The fact that you got to the bottom line quickly indicates that you value your time too. They definitely appreciate this quality in others. You know where you stand with a person like this.

This type of person achieved their present position by sorting out the wheat from the chaff – and that includes the likes of you.

Aggressive: 'What's in it for me?'

Heavy security

You were probably subjected to the third degree before being able to fix up a meeting. You may have had the initial 'Can you write in?' from the secretary or assistant. But your persistence got you through to this person, and they agreed to see you (under sufferance). They emphasized the fact that they couldn't promise anything.

You're guilty until proven innocent

With this type, you're observed suspiciously from the start. You're made to feel very much like an intruder when you enter their domain. This is designed to make you feel uncomfortable. They want the upper hand. They'd like to see you crack. If you're seeing this person with some kind of business proposition, then this would mean you'd probably offer them a better deal, under pressure.

Knows all about you (or so they think)

They claim to know all about you (or your company) from their colleagues, previous dealings and other vague intelligence sources. They actually know very little – but they have these set preconceived ideas. They therefore have a *listening* problem. They're reluctant to give the appropriate attention, and they nod continuously to indicate 'Yes, I know. Yes, I know.' It often turns out that they have confused your company with another, so all their criticism and negative views are directed, wrongly, at you. If you discover this during the meeting and point out the case of mistaken identity, then you risk making them lose face. This type (big ego) cannot cope with that. So you suffer because they couldn't be bothered to check their facts beforehand.

Suffers from desk aggression

Psychologists have long recognized the change that comes over certain people when they get behind the steering wheel of a car ('road rage' is the common term these days). Otherwise thoughtful and kind human beings can become menacing and aggressive in these circumstances.

Put some people behind a large desk and you get an almost parallel situation; let's call it '**desk aggression**'. It gives this type of person a feeling of power and causes a *personality change*. The bigger the desk, the bigger the transformation that takes place.

Try to get this type away from their power base if there's alternative seating (your bad back, the need for a power point for your laptop – any excuse). It could alter the outcome of your meeting.

Looks for ways to trip you up

Basically, they didn't really want to meet with you. But you persisted. So it's a case of 'Come into my parlour for some Chinese torture.'

They'll try to catch you out in what you say. Their ego tells them that whatever they're doing at the moment, they're doing it right. They don't need whatever you're offering. Why introduce another variable into the equation and upset the balance? They're thinking: 'What's in it for me? No thanks. I'll stick with who we've got at the moment. They're not brilliant, but who needs a change?'

Criticizes aspects of your proposition

This type invariably finds fault with aspects of your proposition. It's easier that way. All the time that there is an ego-based justification for sticking with the status quo, they will refuse to accept that the way they have been operating could be improved upon. So they go through all the aspects of your proposal and demolish them. Any valid resistance to their claims on your part is bulldozed.

This type will try to manipulate you from the word go. Keep your cool. They may make concessions if you can maintain your position. The fact that you've refused to budge too much indicates in their eyes that you've got something to offer. Now they're more interested.

General advice for tackling this type of person: use your head (and wear a crash helmet). Be prepared for a few knocks and don't take it personally. Be especially assertive.

Meticulous and methodical

Don't be a minute late

You're dealing with somebody whose life is highly organized. They may be an older person and may have been with the organization for many years. They're very much 'dyed in the wool'.

When you fixed the meeting (for your job interview, presentation, or whatever the circumstances) they were very *specific* about time – 11.40 a.m. for example – and probably insisted on giving you directions. (Even though you told them not to bother as you once worked opposite their offices, they just spoke over you and didn't listen.) Just hear them out. If you don't, you'll offend. Their whole life revolves around *detail*; don't try to change it.

You're due at 11.40 and the meeting will certainly not last longer than 40 minutes. At exactly 12.20, the secretary will come in, like clockwork, with a mug of tea (inscribed with appropriate message: '*When I first stepped out of the womb, on to dry land, I knew I'd made a mistake!*'), and they'll be taking a cheese sandwich and Chelsea bun out of their briefcase as they bid you goodbye.

Doesn't like people who talk fast

Slow down your speech with this type. Things have to be conducted at a certain pace – *their* pace. If you talk fast, they think you're trying to gloss over certain points. This type is more comfortable with people who mirror their verbal and non-verbal behaviour (body language).

Long pauses when they talk to you

This type is generally cautious, including in their choice of words. Consequently, they s-t-r-e-t-c-h everything out, and there are long pauses mid-sentence. It's difficult to know when to start talking because you don't know when they've finished discussing a particular point. If you interrupt them inadvertently, they'll never forgive you. You think they've finished their sentence; then, *just when you thought it was safe to go back into the conversation . . .*

...just when you thought it was safe to go back...

Has done extensive research

It's a by-product of this type's nature that they have to have all relevant facts and assess all possible alternatives before making up their mind on anything.

In your case, that means they've evaluated possible alternatives to your proposition, so you had better be clued up on what you're proposing. They won't tell you what their own research has shown them. That's one of the reasons why they s-t-r-e-t-c-h everything out; there's less chance of them accidentally giving anything away. They've researched other alternatives, they know what else is on offer, and their filing cabinet will testify to that. They hoard information like a squirrel hoards nuts.

Wants straight answers

When they ask you a question, make sure you answer it (this is not the time to practise for a political interview on BBC Radio 4). Their mind is programmed to receive a reply. Without one, their mental 'computer' cannot go on to the next instruction.

Wants everything in writing

After the meeting, they will insist that everything you've discussed be put in writing (hope you made lots of notes). This doesn't necessarily signal interest in your proposition. It is more of a safety valve (for them) should they actually decide to talk to you again.

Unfortunately, the lack of spontaneity in this type means that you rarely get any agreement at an initial meeting. Much of your face-to-face impact is lost because of having to go away and put everything discussed in writing. The sad thing is that this sort of person forgets most of the original discussion and remembers only what is said in the subsequent, often flavourless, letter.

The matter is very much in their hands now. You can't force another meeting, and the best you can hope for is that you're contacted again. So your letter or email has to be effective. Reiterate the good points you made; don't dwell on their unfounded concerns. It's up to them to remember those. Cover most of the important points. Always remember that they're probably going to discuss this with somebody else in the organization – and that person hasn't even seen you.

Calls you back to meet a third party

If they ask you back for another meeting, they will probably bring in somebody else. It may be a person who has a vested interest in your discussion. Their instinct for playing safe means that they want approval from the third party. Or, as is probably more often the case in job interviews and in business, they want to be able to *dilute the blame* if things don't turn out quite right. ('Well, John agreed we should hire him. He was also impressed with the guy's track record' or 'Guy and Andrew thought the proposal was cost-effective compared with . . . ')

Try to work out what type the third party is and handle them accordingly. But remember that the ultimate decision-maker is your original contact, Mr or Ms Methodical. *Aim to get the third party to influence them*. Let them take the reins.

Remember that, essentially, you're dealing with a *pedant* here. If you can recognize this difficult type and have the patience and understanding to cope with them, then you can get results. But make sure that your proposition is sound. This type can be a pain if there is cause for complaint. Have your air ticket and passport ready!

Friendly: 'Let's fix up a meeting'

Very receptive to your phone call

When you first telephone, this type is quite easy-going and pays attention to what you say. If they're interested, they sell you the idea of a meeting between the two of you. (Makes a nice change.)

Calls you by first name on arrival

This type disposes of formalities and, being the friendly sort, immediately calls you by your first name (they may have worked in the USA or have close links there by virtue of the organization they work for). They may ask you to call them by their first name.

Has an unconventional seating arrangement in their office

Their office is very homely; it's an extension of themselves. Their desk and its immediate surrounding area is intended for their use only; it is tucked away at the far corner of the room. They don't like discussions from their desk; it's too territorial and not fair on their visitors. Besides, their current paperwork would prevent them from giving undivided attention to you. This is a godsend for you. You may sit on a couch or comfortable chair – it's all very relaxed. 'Take your jacket off, if you like,' they offer.

Talks a lot initially

When you first meet, this type talks a lot to put you at ease (very common with good interviewers who are assessing job applicants). They speak with animated gestures and facial expressions that say 'I'm enjoying life' and also 'I'm enjoying our conversation' (although you haven't said anything yet!).

Asks you about your personal life

This type just shows a keen friendly interest in you. He or she is a people person; they make no bones about it – they've got good 'people skills' and you're going to benefit from this. Their experience tells them that you're a nice person to deal with (whatever the outcome), so they're finding out more about you. They ask about your hobbies and interests (which you may touch upon quite naturally in the conversation, when you notice their rugby trophy, for example) and look for common ground. They may leave discussion about what you actually came to see them for until much later.

Agrees to your proposition quickly

If they're interested, they like to tell you so almost immediately; they don't believe in playing games once they've made up their mind, one way or the other. You've passed the test. You're on to the next stage with them now, and they want to know what that is. They value *your* time as well as their own.

It's bound to be a pleasure dealing with a person of this type. They invite *empathy* and *sincerity* (they show these themselves), and if you've got it you can hardly fail. They are undoubtedly the ideal type to deal with if your personality matches. There are a few of them around, but they're not that easy to find.

Amicable: 'Let's get you off your guard'

There is a variation on the friendly type that is worth mentioning. Their friendliness is motivated by self-interest – they want to lull you into revealing information.

Pleasant welcome when you arrive

You are greeted by your first name and made to feel like a long-lost friend.

Seating is informal

Similar to the previous type.

Keen to know your 'status'

If you're seeing this person on a business matter, they will study your business card closely; they want to gauge your seniority. They ask how long you've been with your organization (or had your own company, or whatever). They want to know whether you have the clout to make a decision on a deal (that they have carefully thought out before you arrived), or whether you'd have to get approval from someone else back at the office. If they work out that you do have ultimate authority then as well as coffee you'll be offered biscuits.

By establishing your track record, they may just be ensuring that they're dealing with someone experienced. That's quite in order. So they're checking out your credentials, and if they're not happy you may have a very short meeting. ('What? He's only been in the business for three months? I've been in it 28 years; he can't tell me anything! I'll cancel the coffee. Now, where's that ejector-seat button? Goodbye Mister Bond!')

If you feel that your short career within your present organization may make them uneasy in terms of their confidence in you, make sure you allude to your previous experience.

Tries to make you feel relaxed and off-guard

This type knows that in most formal situations where you are visiting somebody (it can even be another person's office in the same building in which you work) it is the *host* who has the territorial advantage.

So, by departing from the norm and making you feel relaxed and open in conversation, they're likely to get a little more out of you – maybe a *lot* more. Who knows, you may even tell them some secrets (office gossip, competitor information). But they could just be testing you. If you reveal things about *them* (competitors) then you may reveal things about *him* or *her*! ('Thanks for the useful information; it'll come in very handy. And by the way – sorry I can't help you.')

This friendly type also knows that if you are relaxed then you're likely to compromise that bit more in a negotiating situation. After all, if the visitor is made to feel well-received, they'll probably make an extra effort.

This type is *calculating*. So make sure that, despite the relaxed surroundings, you remain totally in control. They're hoping to put you in an expansive mood. If you falter at all, they'll seize on this as a chance to take advantage. Remain alert. If they agree to your proposition and you bend a little to make it more attractive to them, let them see it's a *deliberate* decision on your part and not the result of weakening under pressure. They'd rather deal with somebody who is strong-minded.

Most people are a cocktail of different personality types, but certain traits seem to form in '**clusters**', as we noted at the beginning of this chapter. Understanding different behavioural features and mentally classifying those so afflicted (or blessed) will be an enormous aid in using your ESP techniques.

With most types, there is a little bit of another type trying to get out. You can draw this out by your line of questioning. But the techniques you use will also depend on what type you are.

How do you come over?

Let's take a look at a few examples of the behavioural characteristics of some people 'on the other side of the desk'.

Rambles on regardless

On arrival, discusses journey/traffic ad nauseam

This type can't help themselves. They feel compelled to comment on road or weather conditions as an easy opener, either because they are nervous or because they can't think of anything else to say. Also, it provides a convenient opener if they're not comfortable being there.

Of course, it's all right to remark on the ups and downs of your journey, your parking problems and rail cancellations; in fact, the other person may even ask. But it should be kept brief. It isn't the point of the visit.

Carries a large synthetic case

This type's bulging case is offputting. We're into high tech these days, with electronics substituting for bulk. Their case looks like it's just come off the baggage-reclaim carousel. It contains masses of literature, case studies, personnel files, pens, a shoe horn and so on. The sight of this can be an immediate turn-off to the other person, who doesn't want a hard time – they've got time constraints, like everybody else. What's going to come out of this Pandora's box?

Floods the person's desk with papers

This type assumes that the other person is a graduate of the rapid reading school and starts by overloading them with visual material. They've latched on to that old favourite: 'A picture paints a thousand words.' They don't understand about timing and relevance.

Talks while the other person is trying to read

Ugh! It's bad enough for the poor person struggling with the heaps of paper put in front of them. As they try to read, their visitor is wittering away. They don't know what to concentrate on. Should they be listening *and* looking at their visitor, or should they be reading? They can't do both. There is no answer to this one.

Pays no regard to time

This type doesn't attempt to find out how much time the other person has before their next engagement. They ramble on regardless, intent only on the time they have to kill ('I'll stay until it stops raining . . . until the parking meter runs out . . . until 2.35, and then I can catch the 3.10 . . .').

Monotonous and mean with words

Speaks in a monotone

This type is oblivious to the handicap of their dull speaking voice and goes through life inflicting misery on their listeners. With no variation in their speech, they could win a Dalek contest. Because there is no enthusiasm in their voice, if they try to sell themselves or their ideas they are doomed to alienate their audience. On the telephone, their monotone is magnified even more.

Uses a minimum of facial expressions

This type's face shows no warmth or sincerity; they rarely smile. It never occurs to them. They see work, and life itself, as a *serious* business. Since they display scarcely any non-verbal signs of emotion, the other person never knows whether this type is on the same wavelength, or whether they care and understand about their problems and requirements.

Speaks almost from a script

For some uncanny reason, the above type is usually guilty of further aggravating the situation by speaking in a stilted, almost scripted way. You can imagine them at home saying to their partner: '*It's come to my attention that the radiator in the back room is leaking.*'

Their complete lack of empathy and sincerity prevents them from getting inside the other person's mind, identifying their type and tailoring their words accordingly. It's a script – delivered in that characterless voice. Could anything be worse?

They've done it so many times that it follows a set pattern. If the other person comes up with a question or argument that's not in the script, forget it! It's just edited out. There's no room for improvisation.

Often talks over the other person

Watching this happen is quite painful; and when you're on the receiving end, it really hurts. You may see it on TV chat shows and in other interview situations. Talking over the other person's words may be the stock-in-trade of politicians, but in everyday dealings it's very rude.

We are all *occasionally* guilty of talking at the same time as somebody else – in an argument, for example, or if we're excited about something. That's acceptable.

But it's not acceptable in a professional setting, when you're aiming to persuade. You need to know exactly what the other person is saying so that you can formulate a reply, quite apart from manners. The other person won't voice their disapproval (though their body language will give it away, if you're attuned to it); they'll probably just reject you.

Whatever they do in life, people of this type will find it very difficult to relate effectively on an interpersonal level or to get their message across effectively. When they're trying to influence or persuade people to come round to their way of thinking, their chances of success are very low.

Overfamiliar, over the top

Uses first name too soon

This type calls the other person by their first name as soon as contact is made (often on the phone). This issue needs to be addressed. Say you're telephoning a potential client, Nick Peters, for the first time. The secretary puts you through to the boss. If you begin by saying, 'Hi, Nick. It's Tom Smith from Universal Imports speaking,' your forwardness is unlikely to be received well. It's different if you've been referred to Nick by a mutual friend or acquaintance that you know fairly well, and they've suggested that you call him (and maybe even let Nick know to expect a call).

Many people object to overfamiliarity. They might accept your using their first name at the end of conversation, when you've established rapport, but not while you're an unknown quantity. To many people, it immediately spells insincerity. Whatever you say next may be lost.

The first-name approach is an accepted practice in the USA, and although it has gradually crept over to this side of the

Atlantic a traditional British reserve still dictates a certain protocol. So, far safer to remain on a formal footing until you've built up some kind of empathy.

Flatters insincerely

There's nothing wrong with the odd compliment or piece of flattery – if it's meant sincerely. If appropriate, it can be taken as a positive show of interest and set a pleasant mood to a discussion. Insincere flattery could have a much worse effect than labelling you as superficial. It can introduce doubt into the other person's mind: 'If you can flatter me, then you're probably flattering your CV/proposal/etc. So I don't trust you.'

Regards listening as time-wasting

This type goes on speaking without pausing for breath. They believe that silence is a void to be filled – by *them*, not anybody else. After all, they're the one with the proposition, so they should do all the talking. Unfortunately, they've never listened long enough to learn the error of their ways.

Overenthusiastic about their proposal

This type refuses to believe or even consider that there are any possible negative points or flaws in their line of reasoning. They're so obsessed by the common directive to be *positive* (or the flip side – *not* to be *negative*) that they carry it too far. As far as they're concerned, what they're proposing is simply the best. They won't encourage a dialogue that might allow the other parties to voice any objections or concerns, which can then be laid to rest. They don't give them a chance to weigh things up.

Sulks visibly on rejection

When given a thumbs-down verdict, this type of person is mortified ('What? You've made me speak non-stop for the past 45 minutes for nothing? You cannot be serious!').

Instead of analysing the reasons for their non-convincing display, they may aggravate the situation by telling the other person that they drove two hours in the rain to get there, or that they are not impressed by their way of operating, or that they are convinced that the other person is making a big mistake, etc. They thus ruin any chance of the door being left open for future contact.

People can change their minds at a later date. It's natural. We all do. Circumstances change. Life is not static. We may just have caught someone on a bad day.

If you've left the door open and parted amicably, then there may be another opportunity. If you challenge the other person's decision and react badly to losing out, you may burn your boats.

This type of person never establishes any degree of rapport with people generally, and certainly not with business contacts. If they're successful in reaching an agreement with someone, and things don't turn out to the other person's satisfaction, then they will see the same inflexibility and insincerity that they encountered (and excused) when they first met them. Result: loss of goodwill.

Confident and assertive: 'It's in your interest to talk to me'

Acknowledges that other people's time is precious

This type creates a good impression from the first minute by showing that they know other people are busy.

Being inaccessible to all and sundry is equated with status. So, when you acknowledge that somebody has limited time, you're saying between the lines: 'I know you're in demand, and therefore I appreciate you taking time to talk to me (but it's worth it – otherwise I wouldn't be bothering you).' This implication makes the other person more amenable. The other person is a busy individual in an important position that affords them esteem. People respect them; they show that they *appreciate* being given some of their time. (What would we do without ego?)

There is further prestige – for both parties – in letting the other person know that you are busy too. They want to deal with other busy/successful people – like you. It makes you members of the same club. So, let them know your time is valuable by taking the cue for leaving: don't outstay your welcome, and tell them how much time you can spare. You're helping to shape their perspective of you.

Lets the other person pick the pleasantries

In our first dealings with people, we all need some warming up, rather like an athlete preparing for a performance. Your aim is to try to establish some empathy early on. It can be awkward for both parties when you haven't met before (first impressions), but it's worse for you if you're visiting somebody on their home ground. It's a little easier in neutral surroundings.

So, let the other person take the lead on the small talk. If you end up talking about something that they are sufficiently interested in to prolong (and they're enjoying) the discussion, fine. That's what you're there for anyway: to get inside their mind. To find out what makes them tick, what their interests are, what their values are. Everything follows from that. You know that very well from your own experience.

You're showing you're a good listener. People appreciate good listeners. Let them decide when to cut it short.

Makes the person feel comfortable

This is an extremely valuable quality. Most people's attitudes and reactions are shaped by the other person's demeanour. If you are tense then you may make the other person so. If you smile, you'll probably find it's contagious. You're trying to create the right mood, and you want them to be relaxed (because people give more of themselves when they feel this way), so be comfortable within yourself. Look as though you're bent on enjoying the meeting and want to help the other person. With a smile in your voice, you're letting them know that there's no compulsion to accept your message, so they needn't be on their guard. Remember: you're dealing in the art of gentle persuasion.

The other person may be a serious type and may need drawing out. They may just be worried or in a bad mood for some reason. You need them to be in a receptive frame of mind. People will, all things being equal, generally mirror your mood after a while. If the person sitting opposite you is being pleasant, for example, it's hard not to be pleasant back. Be patient. Try it.

Maintains eye contact most of the time

This type of person reads body language well and picks up all the signals. The point is often laboured, but successful negotiators in all walks of life will testify to the fact that the eyes can reveal all.

Watch the eyes the next time you're talking to somebody. When you ask a question and are given a verbal answer, look for the eye message too. We often say one thing and then provide a supplementary answer with our eyes. It can be a valuable way of finding out what somebody is really thinking.

Sincerity shows in our eyes when we feel strongly about something. Similarly, if we're lying or being insincere, an astute person can pick this up.

Maintaining eye contact shows that we are listening. This gives more depth to the conversation. If we look interested, then the other person's interest is sustained. Looking somebody squarely in the eye gives the impression that we're being 'up front'. Spectacle-wearers can have a problem here, incidentally. Light reflected from their lenses (if they haven't been coated) means that the person looking at them may see only rays of light. This is not very helpful for making and maintaining eye contact, and it can be off-putting. Similarly, heavily tinted or dark glasses prevent eye messages being sent (or picked up) so making – and keeping – eye contact thus becomes virtually impossible.

Coffee break . . .

As a clue to the 'type' preference of the person you are interacting with, the golden rule is:

(a) listen to their l_____

(b) observe their b_____.

Although there is diversity b_____ personalities, there is also consistency w____ personalities.

We know that 'i_____' and 'e_____' are opposites, yet most people possess both traits, with one attitude dominant over the other: the dominant one represents c_____ behaviour; the subordinate one represents u_____ behaviour.

Time and time again, research confirms that in our interactions in everyday life (both in and outside work) we are drawn to people with a d_____personality style that is similar to our own. With other people, we adapt our interaction with them based on the t_____ that they exhibit.

Just as when we're looking at 'body language' signals, it's important when trying to ascertain an individual's 'type' that we make an assessment only after observing b_____ in *context*, rather than making snap j_____ out of convenience.

Since success in influencing, or getting people to see your point of view, is often dependent on the measure of r_____ we achieve with the other person – at least in the early stages – knowing whether you are dealing with an 'E' or an 'I', for example, is invaluable.

Your success in identifying and successfully dealing with various 'types' hinges on your e_____ (or mind-reading!) skills.

Identify the type of person you are dealing with; and then adapt your approach so that it addresses the way the other person t____.

Appendix: Coffee break answers

Chapter 2

- talking
- five, ahead
- interrupt
- behind, backs
- thoughts, emotions
- paraphrasing
- sensory, psychological, meaning
- feelings, conveyed, other

Chapter 3

- rising
- breakdown
- admit
- concentration
- said, visual, interruptions
- emotional
- 40
- eyes

Chapter 4

- make, receive
- 45, 55

- paralanguage
- congruent
- eye contact
- gesture
- open
- clusters
- communicate

Chapter 5

- confidence
- rehearse
- associations
- interest
- relationship
- distracted, mind
- empty promises
- attention
- knowledge

Chapter 6

- minds, emotions
- interpretations, interpretation, feeling
- laziness
- defensiveness
- closed
- negative
- best

Chapter 7

- begin
- personality

- words, tone, voice
- happening, interrupting
- Timing, proposition
- When, when not, outcome

Chapter 8

- cooperation, competition
- position
- trustworthiness, honesty
- transient
- interests, needs
- win–win
- listening
- indicate
- after
- concessions

Chapter 9

- expectations, boundaries
- downside, information
- understand, agreeing
- language, analytical
- verification
- exaggeration, lies, behaviour
- emotional intelligence, open-
- awkward
- narcissistic, praising

Chapter 10

- language, behaviour
- between, within

- introversion, extroversion, conscious, unconscious
- dominant, traits
- behaviour, judgements
- rapport
- empathy
- thinks

Oh, by the way. How did you get on with the missing $3 with our three travellers in Chapter 8?

Answer: **There is no missing $3!**

The hotel receptionist has $30 in his safe. The travellers have their $9. The bellboy has $6. That's $45. **Is it any wonder there is often a huge gulf between perception and 'reality'?**

(Be aware when trying to persuade that every person looks at the world through their own filter and therefore has their own perception.)

Scoring scale: PQ (Your Persuasion Quotient)

1 point for each correct answer

95-110	This book must have done you some good.
	Empathy + Sincerity > Persuasion. Your ESP is high.
85–94	Your persuasive skills are developing by the minute.
65–84	Nearly there.
40–64	A few weak areas that need working on.
30–39	Come on – get inside the mind! Please read the book again.
20–29	Maybe it's time to cut out the speed-reading!
19 and below	Don't answer any more questions please, without checking with your *lawyer*!

Afterword

Persuasion is the core skill for survival and success in the modern world, as it was in the ancient world as well for that matter.

James Borg has brought together the latest scientific findings and a host of examples and illustrations to provide a highly readable, *authoritative* and *indispensable* handbook for all of us who need to get other people to do what we want.

Sir Antony Jay

Sir Antony Jay is the writer and creator of BBC's Yes, Minister *and* Yes, Prime Minister, *as well as the original co-founder (with John Cleese) of training films company Video Arts.*

Index

ALSO BY JAMES BORG

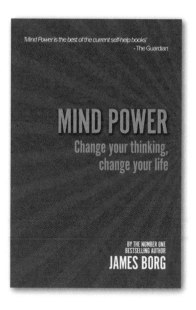

'Mind Power is the best of the current self-help books'
- The Guardian

MIND POWER
Change your thinking, change your life

BY THE NUMBER ONE
BESTSELLING AUTHOR
JAMES BORG

Our thoughts create our reality, so the quality of your thinking determines the quality of your life. *Mind Power* will show you how to free yourself from the thoughts that limit you in your personal and working life. You'll become acutely aware that when you change your thinking – you change your life.

"An author of inspirational works."
– The Independent

".... *Persuasion* and *Body Language* have both been well-received and when you read *Mind Power* it's easy to see why...intelligent and rational ways in which everyone can get their neurons firing and improve their thinking. Light-hearted and enthusiastic style make this one of the better self-help books out there."
– Booksquawk

"Mind Power by James Borg is the best of the current self-help books."
– The Guardian

ALSO BY JAMES BORG

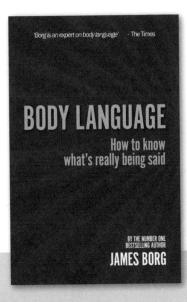

'Borg is an expert on body language' - The Times

BODY LANGUAGE
How to know what's really being said

BY THE NUMBER ONE
BESTSELLING AUTHOR
JAMES BORG

"Borg is an expert on body language."
– The Times

....

"This book shows you how to use your body language to your advantage."
– ShortList magazine (No 1 - 'The Year's Best Business Books' 2009)

....

"Barack Obama was once asked which book he would take to The White House if he became President. His reply was "Abraham Lincoln's" . . . sadly I couldn't think of any which I held in similar esteem. However, James Borg's book starts to address this situation."
– Supply Management magazine

....

"It is definitely a five-star read!"
– San Francisco Book Review

....

"I've become an expert in this field since studying *Body Language*. . . in seven chapters he takes the reader through the shocking ways our bodies reveal boredom, dislike, anxiety, indifference, mendacity – and, in happier moments, liking and even attraction."
– The Independent

Winner of BAA (British Airports Authority)
'Best Non-Fiction Travel Read' Award

(Voted for by the public)